A PECULIAR
TRIBE OF
PEOPLE

A PECULIAR TRIBE OF PEOPLE

MURDER AND MADNESS IN THE HEART OF GEORGIA

RICHARD JAY HUTTO

Lyons Press
Guilford, Connecticut
An imprint of Globe Pequot Press

Lyons Press is an imprint of Globe Pequot Press.

Designed by Sheryl P. Kober
Layout artist: Kevin Mak
Project editor: Kristen Mellitt

Library of Congress Cataloging-in-Publication Data is available
on file.

ISBN 978-1-59921-997-4

Printed in the United States of America

10 9 8 7 6 5 4 3 2 1

CONTENTS

I have found that anything that comes out of the South is going to be called grotesque . . . unless it is grotesque, in which case it is going to be called realistic.

—FLANNERY O'CONNOR

PROLOGUE

On the morning of May 12, 1960, the Burge family maid discovered the body of Mary Burge, dead in her large, canopied bed, carpet fragments lodged under her fingernails from her desperate attempt to claw her way to escape from the murderer. The family physician, Dr. William R. Birdsong, was called immediately, followed soon thereafter by the Bibb County coroner. The medical examiner was notified just before the sheriff, who placed a call to the Burges' only child, John L. Burge, who was then teaching at Auburn University.

Evidently no one thought to call the dead woman's husband.

Chester Burge lay alone at the local hospital recovering from hernia surgery, without receiving any word from the authorities, and when the newly widowed patient heard on the radio the news of his wife's murder, he shouted from his bed and, in what a contemporary called "that high-pitched voice," telephoned his cousins who were staying in Burge's guest cottage. Chester did not arrive at the crime scene (his wife's bedroom) until early afternoon, when he exited an ambulance still clad in light green pajamas and maroon bathrobe. He was carried on a stretcher led by Detective Frank Lanneau through his darkened home, a police photographer close behind, his flash popping brightly. In a shaky voice, Chester told the officer that he had given his wife a wallet containing $5,000 as she was leaving the hospital the previous night, and asked her to take it home.

"We haven't found it," Lanneau told Chester. "So robbery—"

"Did you look under the mattress?" Chester replied.

He was right. The wallet was recovered from between the mattress and box springs, and contained only one dollar and a few assorted papers. A locked closet had been pried and its paint chipped, as though someone had attempted unsuccessfully to open it. Chester unlocked it for Lanneau and determined that their substantial cash, liquor, and valuable papers were intact.

A loaded .38 caliber revolver lay untouched on the bedside table. His wife's jewels, which he had stated openly and on numerous occasions were worth $250,000, were all accounted for—except one diamond clip. Undisturbed on the nightstand was the diamond necklace she had worn to the hospital when she had visited him the night before.

Her ten-carat diamond ring remained on her finger, though the jewel was missing, having been plucked from its mooring. Her killer had battled so strongly to steal the ring that her finger had very nearly been severed from her hand.

The police photographer's flash bulb popped once more, and Lanneau caught a glimmer on the carpet. The diamond from Mary's ring was half-hidden on the floor, tangled in the rug's fibers.

Mary and Chester's most recent wills, written the previous January, sat on the bedroom desk, the seal broken only on Mary's.

Save for the sounds of the photographer and detective, the room was silent. Mary's "big, noisy" pet parrot, who voiced loud warnings when anyone approached, had been found bleeding on the day of Mary's murder and had died at dusk on the night its owner would be killed, carried away only hours before the woman who loved it. The family's setter dog, Boy, had been found a few hours before Chester's arrival, stashed and whimpering in the basement, behind a door locked from the inside.

———

My wife and I moved to Macon in 1993 and had lived in our house only a few days when I first recall hearing the modern moniker for Chester Burge's old mansion—"the murder house," the neighbors casually called it, always in passing. Still elegant even today, the Shirley Hills neighborhood retains an undeniable cachet even though newer money has moved to Macon's northern suburbs. Every day as I turn onto my street, the headlights of my car sweep the lawn of Chester's house on the corner. Like a teenager who was told the dark, abandoned house in the neighborhood is haunted, I was intrigued, drawn toward the mystery of the mansion on the hill.

I'd known Jordan Massee a year when I confessed my strange fascination with the house and my curiosity about the stories that it held. A Macon literary icon, Massee held the history of the city in his fecund mind. In the early twentieth century, Massee's family had served as the literary centerpiece of Macon, hosting writers and artists of varying colors and stripes, even playing host to Tennessee Williams on his visits to Macon. It was under Jordan's influence that Williams finished *Cat On a Hot Tin Roof*, and the author made it clear that Jordan's father, the elder Massee, was the model for Big Daddy. (Jordan's father was rumored to have lost the family mansion in a poker game, which would have made Williams smile: he loved him for his larger-than-life personality.) When *Cat* opened in New York, Jordan and his father were there at Williams's invitation. Later, when Carson McCullers—Jordan's cousin—held her now-famous literary luncheon in New York, playing host to Arthur Miller, Isak Dinesen, and Marilyn Monroe, Jordan was there, too. He was, in fact, the only guest who wrote about the memorable event. When I would visit him in the mid-1990s, there sat on his bookshelf a framed image of that gathering. Dinesen is seated in the center drawing the rapt attention of McCullers while Miller looks over her shoulder, with a handsome young Massee standing behind in the company of angels. A quiet Marilyn rests on the edge of the picture, startling in her beauty but proud to be part of such a learned group even if on its periphery.

Jordan found my interest in Chester Burge's home and history amusing at first, feeding me stories here and there, enticing me with bits of the strange and sordid tale of a family most of Macon would like to forget. He enjoyed sharing a little at a time. It wasn't until he was prompted by a letter from New York that his amusement turned to intensity. A writer from the Northeast wrote Jordan, declaring she was doing research on the trial of Burge with the intention of writing a book, and Jordan came alive. Over cocktails at his house one early evening, he presented to me a scrapbook, filled with clippings from the trial sent to him by his sister while he was living in New York. As he wrote years later in the front of the album, "I made a scrapbook ... so that Carson [his cousin, author Carson McCullers] could read it. This became her favorite murder since Lizzie Borden."

Opening the scrapbook gently, he said to me, "This is a Macon story, and it shall be written by a Macon hand."

And so I began to write the story of Chester Burge. Prompted by Jordan, I would interview residents, visit local libraries and archives, and occasionally find myself trespassing on someone's property or, sometimes, their memory. Always I'd return to Jordan's house with my new stock of notes and questions, and always he'd respond with a new list of names, new clues to the mystery.

It became obvious the saga was like an onion. When various layers were peeled back, more were uncovered. The layers were rarely like Georgia's prized Vidalia onion, noted for its sweetness, but much more offensive to the senses. One matron of an old Macon family beseeched me not to write about Chester as "no one needs to hear about all that." What she really meant was that she didn't want Macon to be embarrassed and ridiculed. Sleeping dogs are better left to die in their sleep. Private misbehavior can be excused and conveniently forgotten, but Chester crossed the line into public revelation and broke that unwritten rule far too many times. However, inconvenient memory or not, no one can deny the existence of court documents and public records that tell a story too bizarre to be written as fiction even if some would prefer they remain undisturbed.

Newspaper records disclosed that, only two weeks before the murder, reporters had assembled at the Burge house when Ku Klux Klansmen descended upon the property to protest Chester's renting homes in white neighborhoods to black families. Known as a slumlord in Macon and beyond, Burge sold shotgun houses to blacks, attaching mortgages with reversionary clauses—when one payment was missed, the house once again became Burge's, freeing him to resell it to another unsuspecting black buyer. Chester even owned the Walton, Macon's best-known black hotel, although he was anything but an integrationist; the only color that mattered to him was green. On the night of the Klan demonstration, more than two hundred spectators gathered near the Burge home, watching the procession of white robes emerge from the dark Macon night. The Klansmen had planned to illuminate an electric cross in Chester's yard but could find no electric outlet to supply power.*

---

* By an ironic twist, the Klan had protested at the house years before when it was owned by a newspaper publisher who had been thought too "pro-Negro," a term that could not accurately be applied to Chester.

On the evening of the protest, the family chauffeur had been given a traffic citation, having turned so quickly into the driveway that he barely missed two men, who demanded the police arrest him. Chester stood on the porch holding a gun, while Mary walked out briskly, perched herself upon a stone wall, and began chatting with the Klansmen, assuring them that she would convince her husband to rent only to whites in the area in question. Softened by her intervention, the Klan's Grand Dragon walked up to the house and spoke to Chester, who assured him that, if he could find a white family to rent the property, the black family would be evicted immediately. As quickly as they had gathered, the Klansmen decamped.

Mary's murder just two weeks later brought fresh attention to the Burge home, which had by this time gathered unto itself a reputation. Newspapers from as far as Atlanta sent reporters, who wrote of the Burges' "lavishly furnished" residence. Even for Atlanta papers, a murder story of this kind was big news, supplanting the messy divorce trial of tobacco heir R. J. Reynolds being held on Georgia's coast. Readers of the *Atlanta Constitution* were given detailed reports of developments, including the news that the Burge chauffeur, maid, and former chauffeur, all of whom were black, had been detained for questioning by the police—without benefit of bail or attorney.

Chester, however, returned to the hospital, where he was to undergo more surgery to remove cancerous skin growths. From his bed, he and his son offered a $5,000 reward for information leading to the arrest and conviction of Mary's murderer. On Saturday morning, two days after the death of his wife, he briefly left his hospital bed to attend Mary's funeral services at tony Christ Episcopal Church downtown. The list of honorary pallbearers, including the mayor and several scions of old Macon, was one Chester never could have achieved except under such extraordinary circumstances. While the choir sang and the minister spoke, three more blacks were arrested as material witnesses. Police announced that the Burges' chauffeur had once served nine years in a Michigan prison for having killed his former wife.

It was not until several days after the funeral that police began to intimate that there were motives other than robbery in the murder, and that the suspect pool had been widened.

While the chauffeur and maid submitted to a polygraph test, but then continued to be held, Chester, still hospitalized, refused to do so. The Burges' son, John, resigned his teaching post at Auburn University so that he could establish residency in Georgia to serve as executor of his mother's estate. He, his wife, Jo-Lynn, and their infant daughter, Mary-Leita, immediately moved into his parents' Macon home. Their seven-year-old son, John Lee, already lived there and had been asleep in his room down the hall when his grandmother was murdered. The younger Burge couple moved into the bedroom where his mother had been murdered. Chester's bedroom adjoined Mary's with a shared bathroom.

When the dead woman's will was filed for probate, it revealed that she had left her estate—estimated at half a million dollars—to be divided evenly between her son and husband. The late Mrs. Burge was clear in her stipulations: All taxes and costs were to be deducted from her son's half, while the house was to be included in her son's inheritance. The will stated that she had not chosen her husband to act as executor because she wanted to "relieve him of the many labors, cares, and responsibilities of those positions." The language was euphemistic. Legal records indicated that Chester Burge had been declared legally incompetent on November 20, 1922, and not restored to competence until a legal hearing on May 5, 1956. During all the intervening years, his many properties had been placed in his wife's name.

While the matters of estate were proceeding, the police investigation was moving slowly. Though they claimed to be working sixteen hours a day on the case, the police had made no breaks, and reporters pressed impatiently for any news. In the absence of any, they turned to Chester, who announced that he planned to leave Macon on May 29 and board a cruise ship to Europe a week later.

"I'm not sure now," he told a reporter in a voice weakened from illness, "if I'll be able to go or not, since all this . . . terrible business has come up."

His uncertainty was not feigned. Upon his release from the hospital, he was taken directly to police headquarters, still in pajamas and robe—now a kind of caricature wardrobe—to be questioned and fingerprinted. Because he was unable to climb steps, he was carried in a chair up to the detectives' office. For more than four hours he was questioned, much of that time accompanied by his chauffeur, who was still being held and interrogated. Afterward, he was not taken home to prepare for a sea voyage but was returned to the Macon Hospital—this time to the psychiatric ward at police direction. A guard was posted outside his door.

While Chester was boarded at the hospital, police announced the extension of the investigation to New Jersey, where they were questioning another person of interest (they avoided the language "suspect"). On the evening of the murder, Chester had apparently received two male visitors whom hospital spokesmen had described as "questionable-looking characters." One white and one black, they were remembered because they arrived after the 9:00 p.m. visitors' curfew.

On Wednesday, May 25, two weeks after the murder, while the Burge chauffeur and former chauffeur continued to be held "on open charges," Macon's afternoon newspaper blared the headline BURGE GETS DOSE OF HYPNOTIC DRUGS. Under the care of physicians and a psychiatrist, Chester had been administered scopolamine and amytal—commonly referred to as "truth serum." On May 30, reporters watched police escort a handsome young man into headquarters for questioning. Identified as the man they had interrogated in New Jersey, police insisted that he had come voluntarily, at their invitation.

Finally, on May 30, nearly three weeks after the murder, police arrested Chester Burge.

He had somehow left his hospital bed undetected, police alleged, on the night of his wife's murder. He had made his way to their home, slipped into the house unseen by family and neighbors, and strangled Mary Burge in her bedroom. Then he had returned to the hospital, snuck back into his room on the sixth floor, and feigned ignorance until he heard the police report on the radio. All of this activity, immediately following surgery, was presumably accomplished using six flights of stairs in either direction, without being seen or heard by anyone, and after having been administered two doses of sedatives. When pressed by reporters, police insisted they could prove without a doubt that he had been in his home anywhere from forty-five minutes to two hours.

That, they claimed, was how Chester Burge murdered his wife.

And why? "Because," the police announced vaguely, "she interfered with his private life."

At this revelation the citizens of Macon felt compelled to relate to police and reporters (without attribution, of course) every possible unflattering story about Chester. He may have been a cousin of the Dunlap family, whose mansions dotted College Street, but even they would not receive him. He had finally seduced an elderly Dunlap cousin into his confidence, and she died at his home a mere three days after she signed her new will benefiting him and his family. And, perhaps worst of all, Chester had served a year and a day in a federal penitentiary after pleading guilty to a charge of repeatedly selling whiskey during Prohibition. This was, by any standard, an unusual family, or as Chester's attorney eventually was to call them, "a strange tribe of people."*

On June 5, 1960, the Bibb County grand jury delivered two indictments against Chester Burge, the first for the murder of his wife. While it was a terrible shock to Macon's gentry to learn that one of their own—albeit one as marginalized as Chester Burge—could have killed his wife, it was the second indictment that astounded middle Georgia in the pre–Civil Rights summer of 1960. For in that count, which described the event in exact detail, Chester Burge was charged with having committed sodomy with his black chauffeur, Louis Roosevelt Johnson, who was not charged with any crime.

---

* Even though the newspapers reported the comment as "a strange tribe of people," one juror emphatically remembered it as "a peculiar tribe of people." There is no trial transcript. During the trial, a prosecutor also referred to "a peculiar love, a mighty dangerous love." I chose to use *A Peculiar Tribe of People* as an apt and appropriate title for this book.

CHAPTER ONE

The heavy velvet draperies in Miss Pink's Macon home held out the sun just as surely as their owner held out against any concession to the modern world. The ancient family retainer, Leila, who appeared to be as old as her mistress, still waited upon the doyenne and her guests. Miss Pink reigned over her dinner table while, girlishly and monochromatically dressed, she coyly smiled down at me, an impressionable law student who had always been more comfortable in Miss Pink's era than in his own.

I didn't dare pick up my fork until Miss Pink did, and as she showed no sign of doing so, I sat attentively while our mutual friend prompted her to relate stories that were by then well-known to him. As she lost her train of thought, she would turn expectantly and say sweetly to our friend, "And what did I do then?"

"Something marvelous," he'd reply as he refreshed her memory.

Hattie Tracy King Hartness, called "Pink" her entire life because of a steadfast devotion to the only color she would wear, often crossed College Street as a girl and walked up the block to the beautiful white-columned mansion of Lillian Dunlap Stevens. There the older woman, who had every treasure except a child of her own, would read aloud to Pink as they sat on the veranda tightly hugging three sides of the house.

One day a neighbor related a bit of gossip to Pink's mother, within hearing of the little girl, about Pink's own cousin. Pink walked to Mrs. Stevens's house and, after listening to her reading for a while, conveyed the tale. When Mrs. Stevens told her that the story wasn't true, an incredulous Pink asked, "Do you mean she told a lie?"

The older woman only smiled and replied, "Pink, if people believed half of what she said, Macon would be nothing but a boiling cauldron."

When I knew Miss Pink, she was well into her eighties and was still living in the house on College Street in which she was conceived and brought into this world—the sole survivor of three well-born King sisters with a distinguished lineage. Although she lived in her adult years in a home in Starkville, Mississippi, furnished with Miss Lillian's gilded French furniture, she remained part of each year in those familiar surroundings on College Street among her family's things. While she spoke, I glanced at the imposing silver compote on her sideboard, monogrammed with the initials "LDS." It had, like many of the furnishings in the house, been left to her by the same Lillian Dunlap Stevens who warned her about Macon's propensity to exaggeration—an affliction shared, if not exceeded, by most of its Southern counterparts. Having grown up in Savannah, I had always looked upon Macon as some sort of poorer country cousin: nice to visit for brief interludes when one felt somewhat charitable. No one taught me such a prejudice—surely not my parents—but it was there just the same. My mother moved to Savannah as a young bride and soon subscribed to the belief that its residents were much like the Chinese: They ate a great deal of rice and they worshipped their ancestors. Until I entered law school and took up residence on College Street directly across the street from the imposing mansion earlier owned by Lillian Dunlap Stevens, Macon was little more to me than a stopping point on the way to Atlanta. And by then the Dunlap mansion had become a restaurant. The past was past, it seemed.

Macon doesn't suffer the inferiority complex of Augusta, whose inhabitants always seem so envious of Savannah, nor the edifice complex of Columbus whose architecture can make little claim to rival that of its sister cities. Modern Atlanta, where General Sherman was so careless with a match, embraces its hubris, and it is increasingly difficult to find any natives there except those huddled together in a few ancient gathering places, content in their belief they could still repel the Visigoths who long ago took control. If Savannah has become, in life imitating literature, merely a staging area for John Berendt's book, *Midnight in the Garden of Good and Evil*, then Atlanta relishes itself as the embodiment of Tom Wolfe's *A Man in Full*. It is a sort of Houston, Texas, but with manners and bloodlines. And what of the Georgia of Margaret Mitchell's *Gone With the Wind*? If it survives at all, it seems relegated to a long-abandoned movie set stored somewhere in the suburbs. While the white-columned mansions still exist, either they survive as restored and expensive bed-and-breakfasts, or, as is far more likely, they rise as neo-McMansions on postage stamp–size lots in modern neighborhoods with such marketable names as Tara Estates or Smoke Hill Rise.

Macon's near neighbor, Eatonton, produced both Joel Chandler Harris, who made famous the Uncle Remus tales of Brer Rabbit and Brer Fox, and *The Color Purple*'s Alice Walker, and Macon shares that seemingly incongruous mélange. Where else but Macon can boast Little Richard, Otis Redding, and even Lena Horne for part of her childhood, and yet also offer as native sons The Allman Brothers (whose first album cover was photographed on the steps of the Dunlap mansion) and half of the band R.E.M.? Such curious mixtures must be understood if one can hope to fathom the enigma of Macon, Georgia.

Such distinctions, however, would not have concerned Miss Pink. This was home, and that was all she needed to understand. I did not know then that the mahogany dining table on which we were eating was a gift from Lilly Dunlap Stevens, as were some of the furnishings, which seemed grander than the Victorian home that now held them. Even Miss Lilly's famous jewels—the Dunlap sisters were always known for their impressive jewelry—had been left to Miss Pink.

But not the money. While the Dunlaps were generous in their bequests to friends, the family capital was inviolate. It was passed from sibling to sibling until no more Dunlaps remained.

And therein lay the opportunity for one Mr. Chester Burge.

Miss Pink finally took up her dilatory fork. Her first bite, however, brought the response, "But it's cold!", and she stretched her leg to reach the servant's bell hidden under her foot. Her trusted servant Leila (who would end her days murdered by her own granddaughter—but that is a separate tale) emerged and returned the food to the kitchen. Finally dinner was adjudged to be acceptable, capped by homemade sherbet served at a soupy consistency in Miss Lilly's silver compote, and accompanied by "just a bit of sherry wine" according to Miss Pink, who professed never to have tasted it before this one special occasion. A claim she was to make each time I saw her, she seemed to believe it anew with each telling.

Eventually, not too long after my dinner with her, Miss Pink's jewelry would be doled out one by one to those who preyed upon her in her declining months, with the last several pieces stolen by her nursing aide during her final illness. The house, left to two young men who loved her in her dotage and laughed anew at her stories, would be sold, and some of the neighboring mansions on College Street repeatedly altered in a pattern that mirrored Macon's post-War evolution: first divided into apartments, then adapted for commercial use, and finally torn down in a misdirected attempt at progress.* And so the Dunlaps rest forgotten, though in permanent splendor, in their expensive mausoleum, the first inside the gates of Macon's historic Rose Hill Cemetery. It is an end that would have been unthinkable to the founder of the clan, Captain Samuel S. Dunlap, with whom the story of Chester Burge truly begins.

———

After the War Between the States, old money in Macon had evaporated like rainwater in July. Certainly there was a spring or two remaining—William Butler Johnston, former comptroller/treasurer of the Confederacy's Public Depository (established in 1863 because Macon was adjudged more secure than Richmond), still lived in his Italian Renaissance Revival mansion, which was rumored to hold what remained of the Confederate gold. But for the remaining populace all their Confederate bonds and currency were rendered useless by General Lee's forced capitulation. They remained nothing more than souvenirs of a grand gesture gone hideously awry.

Unlike the well-known northern captains of industry who had almost to a man hired seconds to take their place in the

---

* Two of the Dunlap mansions on College Street survive intact as does their father's house on High Street.

War, the aristocracy of the South would not have dreamed of such a demurrer.* Such a surrender of duty would have brought certain disgrace for a Southerner. And the result of such gallantry? The decimation of the educated gentry of the South. The old families lost their sons, brothers, fathers. For most, only a grievous honor proudly worn as a permanent funeral shroud remained.

Those who made it back walked home nursing their wounds, many of which were invisible. My own great-great-grandfather, John William Jones, shot through the thigh at Petersburg, spent the remainder of the War at Point Lookout, Maryland, a prison that rivaled Georgia's own Andersonville in its squalor and deprivation, with his wounds untreated. He walked home to Georgia after the War and, although a farmer, he refused for the remainder of his life to wear blue overalls, the color of the Northern army.

The end of the War brought not only the purposeful destruction and humiliation of Reconstruction[†] but also the opportunity for advancement for those willing to risk the disdain of their peers. The Southern prototype, Scarlett O'Hara, incurred scorn and ridicule, and a resulting fortune, by her willingness to trade with unscrupulous carpetbaggers and to employ methods of which her proud father would never have approved. For those willing to take such risks, the rewards could be great.

Samuel Scott Dunlap was such a man. Though never a scalawag who cooperated with the hated carpetbaggers, Dun-

* J. P. Morgan continued to stay in touch with his hired replacement and to keep him on the payroll for years as a talisman of the luck he had brought to his master.

† Generally agreed to be one of the most grievous misnomers in the history of domestic affairs.

lap was an example of the "New South," forsaking agriculture for commerce after the War. Born in humble circumstances in rural Jasper County, Georgia, in 1830, Dunlap and his ambitions could not be constrained by such narrow parameters and, recognizing the opportunities afforded by a larger town, he moved to Macon in November of 1849 and accepted a job as clerk in a grocery store for $96 per year, with board. That meager income he saved ferociously, and after three years he entered his own hardware partnership that would become Johnson & Dunlap.

When the War came, he volunteered for the Confederate Army and served for six months as a first lieutenant before resigning that commission to return to Macon and assemble his own company. So successful was he in business that he had sufficient resources to outfit his entire company at his own cost. He went to the front as a captain of the Bibb County Cavalry and fought in the Battles of Second Manassas, Harpers Ferry, and Sharpsburg. Wounded by a Federal officer in hand-to-hand combat at Gettysburg, Dunlap was sent to the Richmond Hospital and then home to Macon to recuperate. For his gallant service he would forever be known as Captain.

In 1864, as Macon was sending small arms, cannon, and supplies to the Confederate Army in Atlanta, Northern troops under the command of General Sherman were dispatched on their infamous march to the sea to break the back of the South. On July 30, 1864, General George Stoneman's troops were approaching a defenseless Macon, intent on freeing Union soldiers in Macon's Camp Oglethorpe and then at Andersonville some seventy miles to the south. Stoneman occupied Captain Dunlap's country home, known as Dunlap's Hill, to serve as his headquarters and from there plan his attack on Macon.

He had seriously underestimated the few men and boys left to defend their hometown. The still-ailing Sam Dunlap rode out from Macon as a scout and came so close to the enemy troops at Clinton that he was discovered and barely succeeded in escaping capture. Dunlap was able to make it back to Macon and report to General Cobb the location of the approaching army. Cobb moved all available troops to the eastern location Dunlap advised, and thus Stoneman's raid was successfully repelled. General Stoneman went on to Griswoldville and Sunshine Church before he found himself imprisoned at the same Camp Oglethorpe he had intended to liberate. He was the highest-ranking Union officer to be captured in the War, and his men were sent to Andersonville prison.*

Meanwhile, Sherman's remaining troops spread their devastation throughout the soon-to-be-conquered Georgia. Burge Plantation near Covington, owned by cousins of Captain Dunlap's wife, was ruled by the widow of Captain Thomas Burge. She was Dolly Sumner Lunt Burge, originally from Maine and a cousin of well-known abolitionist Charles Sumner, and she witnessed the savage raping of the Burge Plantation. (Her diary's first-person account of Sherman's army leaves little doubt for those revisionist historians who insist that Northern troops destroyed only military targets.)

Those troubles were visited upon Macon within days when the same troops who burned Burge Plantation appeared with similar aims. Planned by the North to serve only as a

---

* Macon's only ill-effect of the Battle of Dunlap Hill was that a cannonball fired across the river, aimed at the home of Confederate Treasurer William Butler Johnston, instead hit the home of Judge Asa Holt. Today's visitors to the home, now a museum, can still see the cannonball. General George Stoneman, whose roommate at West Point was future Confederate General Thomas J. "Stonewall" Jackson, was governor of California from 1883 to 1887.

diversionary tactic to move General Sherman's main troops through central Georgia, the attack failed—partially because the bridge over the Ocmulgee was out and the Home Guard was reinforced by troops who happened to be passing nearby. Macon was ready this time, having installed a twelve-pound Napoleon gun and eight others at an earthwork on the Dunlap farm. As a Union cavalryman later wrote, the Southern guns " . . . were in a redoubt, completely blocking the road, there being room only for two horses to enter the works abreast . . . Seeing that the guns could not be removed, and that there was barely time to withdraw the regiment before the rebel infantry would be upon us, I ordered the column to retire under fire from enemy guns."[*]

Thus Macon was spared.[†] And the Dunlap family's place secured—for a time. Captain Dunlap, given partial credit for saving Macon from Sherman's troops under Stoneman's command, was declared a legitimate hero. Needless to say, his subsequent business career was greatly enhanced as a result. Eventually he was able to buy out his partner and operate his hardware business, the S. S. Dunlap Company.

But his wisest decision may have been made prior to such heroics: his choice of a wife. At a time when few women were afforded an education, Wesleyan College in Macon was established in 1836 as the first college in the world to grant degrees to women. Dunlap's future wife, Mary Ann Eliza Burge, was nine years younger than he and already a student at Wesleyan, where girls could matriculate as young as their early teens. She entered

---

[*]   National Park Service: http://www.nps.gov/archive/ocmu/Civil-War.htm.

[†]   To that good fortune, as well as an eventual lack of funds to enable the misguided construction of new buildings, does Macon owe its intact downtown. Macon has more historic districts than any city in Georgia including 6,000 buildings.

her preparatory studies in 1851 and was a college freshman at the age of fourteen in the fall of 1853. Dunlap's marriage into such a family with the will and means to send their daughter to college was definitely an upward move for the clever young man whose background could not equal his bride's. Sam and Mary were given as a wedding present by her family the large farm east of Macon that was called Dunlap's Hill and would be so integral to Macon's survival of the War.* While Sam worked at his hardware business, Mary ran the farm's dairy and, according to some, delivered milk on a cart pulled by dogs.†

Captain Dunlap became a pillar of Macon's Mulberry Street Methodist Church and at his death was its longest-enrolled member. The Dunlaps' first child was born on his father's twenty-seventh birthday in 1857. Named for his maternal grandfather, John Lee Dunlap lived barely past his seventh year. Sam and Mary's six daughters came next (Daisy died as an infant) and, finally, a son to bookend the brood.

Armed with money and education, the girls were suited for fortunate marriages, and they did not disappoint their parents. The fact that none married Macon boys can perhaps be attributed to their wider ambitions or, more accurately, to the fact that the Dunlaps were never completely accepted by what passed for Macon society. Maybe it was their mother's having driven a dogcart, perhaps jealousy that they were among the few Macon families with money after the War, or merely something intrinsic that made them unacceptable. For whatever rea-

---

* Their modest home, spared because it served as General Stoneman's headquarters, still stands at the entrance to the grounds of the National Park Service's Ocmulgee Indian Mounds, where it was until recently the home of the park superintendent and his family.

† That experience was later cited as a reason to deny her access to the social position to which her husband's new-found wealth should have entitled her.

son, the Dunlaps were never embraced by Macon society.* As Miss Pink said of them, "to the manner born they were not."

They would build a grand narrative nonetheless. Clara, the fourth daughter of Captain and Mrs. Samuel Dunlap, would come to play an integral part in the saga of Chester Burge. She was a Philomathaen at Wesleyan—the forerunner of Phi Mu sorority—where she graduated in 1884. Clara married a partner in the chemical firm Charles Pfizer and Company, converted to the Episcopal church, joined the Daughters of the American Revolution and the Daughters of the Confederacy, and moved to New England. But the youngest daughter, Ilah, was the most resourceful. Although her sisters graduated from Wesleyan College (Nettie in 1875, Florine in 1878, Lillie in 1882, and Clara in 1884), Ilah attended Wesleyan but graduated from Salem Female Academy and College in North Carolina.† Considered a great beauty, she must have been viewed by

---

* At least two Maconites from old families who remember them well agree. Says one, "It wasn't because they were new money—the only money that existed in Macon then was new." Laura Nelle O'Callaghan, still vibrant into her nineties, lived in Shirley Hills for more than sixty years and said of the family, "Everyone said the Dunlaps were from the wrong side of the tracks, but I thought that was just ridiculous in Macon. Well, they wanted to be introduced into society. They were too good for anybody . . . They thought they were just the greatest people . . . They had many airs but they were very nice."

Jack Caldwell, who now lives in the College Street home where both Nettie Dunlap Wortham and, later, her sister, Clara Dunlap Badgley, once held court, clearly remembers a conversation he had with his neighbor across the street, Miss Pink, who agreed that the Dunlaps were never socially accepted. She told him that Captain Dunlap "was a merchant and he was from across the river. That shouldn't have made any difference, but it did."

† A few decades later, the famous Soong sisters also graduated from Wesleyan. Ai-ling would marry the richest man in China, H. H. Kung, while sister Ching-ling would marry Sun Yat-Sen, President of the People's Republic of China and the father of modern China. Youngest sister Mei-ling entered Wesleyan at the age of fifteen but graduated from Wellesley, then became the most famous sister as Madame Chaing Kai-Shek, wife of the President of the Republic of China.

her older siblings as their best opportunity for success. She did not look far for a husband, marrying a much older successful planter from nearby Milledgeville. The twenty-one-year-old Ilah married the sixty-six-year-old Colonel Leonidas A. Jordan, a childless widower,* one of central Georgia's largest landowners, and a founder of the Middle Georgia Railroad. Jordan, who lent Georgia's provisional government (at 7 percent interest) the money to keep it afloat immediately after the War, was said to be one of only two men in the South during Reconstruction who could write a check for one million dollars and possess the capital to have it honored. Although his bank account must have made him a highly desirable matrimonial catch, Captain Dunlap was not willing to let his youngest prize out of her family without something unheard-of in Macon—a marriage contract signed the night before the wedding guaranteeing that Ilah would receive all his vast fortune.†

Perhaps the Dunlaps had pretensions to nobility, for this was the era of highly publicized weddings of American heiresses sacrificed on the matrimonial altar to impoverished European titles. The decade of Ilah Dunlap's wedding was the apex of these transatlantic alliances, as great publicity was afforded to the exchange of dollars for titles. In the Dunlap-Jordan marriage, however, it was the groom who held the fortune, which must have made him suitable to Captain Dunlap, who, no doubt, drove a hard bargain for his youngest daughter. But the Captain's hand was to reach even further into the marriage. When the newly married couple left for one month in

---

* His first wife, whom he married in 1868, was Julia Hurt (1842–91), daughter of Early Hurt.

† One of the Dunlap sisters' fellow Macon belles was Nanaline Holt, born in 1869 (the same year as Clara Dunlap), who attended Wesleyan, married James B. "Buck" Duke in 1907, and in 1912 became the mother of tobacco heiress Doris Duke. Nanaline Holt's family home is still occupied in Macon.

New York City before an extended European honeymoon, the bride's younger brother, Sam Dunlap Jr., accompanied them.

Upon their return, Colonel Jordan remodeled the Nathan Beall House at 315 College Street for his young bride, and she furnished it lavishly. His money held out longer than his health. In less than five years, the beautiful young Mrs. Jordan was a very wealthy widow. Her mother and young Sam, the same brother who had accompanied her on her honeymoon, moved into Ilah's College Street mansion. Ilah gave her brother not only her house but one of her late husband's plantations in south Georgia, and helped her sister Clara purchase an adjoining plantation. When Lilly Dunlap Stevens's husband died, she moved from her own home at 267 College Street, now demolished, into her sister Ilah's house, where she presided with her mother and brother. Their other sister, Nettie Dunlap Wortham, had her own mansion, now known as the Caldwell residence, farther down College Street.

Their proximity in Macon was not the group's only expression of family solidarity. Three of them soon owned adjoining plantations in rural Lee County, near Albany, Georgia. Ilah inherited Oakwood, her husband's four-thousand-acre plantation there, complete with a Lutyens-style country home and dependencies. Her siblings soon presided over their own acreage in the area, creating a "family compound" long before the practice became fashionable. At their rural idyll, the Dunlaps retreated from the cares of the world, which in their case consisted of receiving stock dividends and lamenting their continued lack of social acceptance. As one Maconite remembers, their money made them a force to be reckoned with, but their force was economic, not social.

And then the family founder, the Macon legend, Captain Samuel S. Dunlap, died on March 8, 1902. His death was front-page news. The afternoon newspaper carried a photograph of him with the headline MACON MOURNS LOSS OF PROMINENT CITIZEN. The doors of both the Exchange Bank and the Union Savings Bank were draped in black, and their offices closed in respect of their vice president. His out-of-town daughters had been called to Macon, and his wife and children were at his side when he departed the earth and left his land and name to those circling his bed.

His funeral was nothing short of a tearful holiday and a somber parade, impressive both for its size and its display of influence. The body was escorted from his home on High Street by the board of stewards of Mulberry Street Methodist Church, the Macon cavalry company, the employees of the Dunlap Hardware Company, and the directors and employees of both banks with which he was associated. Not only were the doors of Dunlap Hardware closed for the day, but the competing two establishments, Etheridge & Baker and the Merritt Hardware Company, suspended business as well. Prominent among the floral displays were five white wreaths from his daughters amid a "purple mass of violets." The Captain's pallbearers were the undisputed business leaders of the day. One, C. L. Bartlett, would eventually host President Taft in his Tattnall Square home when Macon received one of several presidential visits. Another pallbearer, Augustus O. Bacon, was Georgia's United States senator from 1895 to 1914.*

Without her father's hand to guide her, the beautiful and very wealthy young Ilah almost made a tragic mistake. Ilah's

---

* At Senator Bacon's death, he left his home, "Baconsfield," and its surrounding acreage as a public park and recreation area for the "white women and children" of Macon. Decades later, ensuing civil rights laws made that stipulation illegal and, in a decision that went all the way to the United States Supreme Court, the property reverted to his heirs and was commercially developed. Even today, the park is remembered by some with great fondness for an era of segregated gentility.

account books confirm that she always kept at least one-half million dollars in liquid assets at any time in addition to her extensive stock holding and real estate. Rich young widows were particularly susceptible to fortune hunters who held some claim either to a noble title (often impoverished) or power. Ilah fell under the sway of Luis F. Corea, the Nicaraguan ambassador to the United States who was head of his country's mission. She wrote from Paris to her family to inform them that she and the ambassador would be married at her Macon home on November 1, 1904. But dark accusations were made, among them that her swarthy South American fiancé was not a Spaniard. When the wedding date had come and gone, it was left to Ilah's brother-in-law, Claude M. Badgley, to issue a statement that "the attacks made upon Luis F. Corea . . . evidently inspired by malice, were absolutely false and had no weight upon Mrs. Jordan and her family, who had had for some time in their possession documents from the most reliable sources which left no doubt in their minds as to the ancestry, honor, and standing of Señor Corea in his own country and abroad." The ambassador issued a public challenge to a duel with anyone casting aspersions upon his character, then secured a suite in New York City's Waldorf-Astoria Hotel the following January, where Ilah arrived with her sister Clara for the postponed nuptials. But Ilah must have come to her senses as the wedding never took place.* Instead Ilah was to marry in 1906 at her brother's Macon home an Atlanta attorney, John D. Little,

---

* Ambassador Corea wed instead in 1907 another wealthy young American heiress, India Bell Fleming, whose mother was a second cousin of Nancy Hanks, the beloved stepmother of Abraham Lincoln. U. S. Secretary of State Elihu Root attended the ceremony. In 1916 the ambassador would be party to a bizarre robbery at which a group of six men befriended by a handsome young Mexican were supposedly bound and robbed while guests at an all-male dinner party in New York City.

formerly Speaker of the Georgia House of Representatives from 1898–1901.*

With the death of the head of the Dunlap family in 1902, Samuel Jr., the only son, was thrust into the forefront. His father's will made certain that young Sam would have a majority control of the business even though the eldest Dunlap daughter's husband had been at the company almost from its inception. Young Sam was known as articulate and well traveled. He had a plantation near those of his sisters in south Georgia and traveled so frequently to Europe that he was a welcomed guest at any dinner on his journeys.

Before "Deacon" James Ray (so called because he proudly held that position in his African-American church) came to work for the wealthy Massee family, he was employed by young Sam Dunlap and his mother when they lived on College Street. Jordan Massee remembers Deacon's telling him that the Dunlaps had "great mastiffs—giant dogs. They were fairly ferocious. Two of them knocked the old lady down and scratched her face up, so Sam made her wear a black veil until the scars had healed. He told her to stay upstairs if they had company. We weren't sure if that was because of the scars or because he wanted Mama out of sight like Marcel Proust did his parents. My parents thought it was the latter."

Sam was a sometime-host for his mother and wealthier sister. But he was missing one important ingredient. Alone among the Dunlap children, Sam was unmarried. It was unusual for someone of his stature not to have a wife, and it was also cause for rumor. Both then and now there were insinuations that he shared his sisters' interest in men. It had

---

* He was a named partner in what is now the Atlanta law firm of Powell, Goldstein.

often been said that Sam Jr. hosted Oscar Wilde when he visited Macon.

But there was a different and seemingly incongruous rumor about Sam, equally as shocking and in the final result far more important. It was whispered that he was the father of an illegitimate child, a boy born to a married woman in Macon on January 31, 1904. The mysterious boy would eventually become so enmeshed in the financial dealings of the last of the Dunlap sisters that it was only natural to assume that he must be their illegitimate nephew. That was far more plausible than the explanation that he was, by law, their first cousin once removed. There would never have been any thought of his being received by Miss Pink, no matter how close she had been to the Dunlap sisters, although she was certainly aware of his existence.

The boy legally was the great-grandson of Mary Burge Dunlap's parents. He would one day own one of the great Dunlap properties, "Listenin' Hill," formerly part of Clara and Ilah's compound in southwest Georgia. He would live not far from the mansions on College Street that had served as Dunlap homes for a century. And eventually the long and spidered family would draw back into itself, and the name that began with the marriage of a brave, beloved Captain and a well-educated Wesleyanne would be left to a slumlord and a liquor runner, a man whose wife was strangled in her bedroom while she clawed desperately for her life.

The boy was Chester Burge.

CHAPTER TWO

At 5:30 p.m. on August 20, 1912, Charley Burge had finished up a day's plumbing work at the home of DeWitt McCrary and began walking through the Macon humidity to his wife and son, Chester, who awaited him at home. Just past A. T. Small's store on Main Street in east Macon, he stepped off the curb without noticing an oncoming car. Witnesses say he tried to jump back but was struck by the automobile, which stopped immediately, with Charley Burge pinned partly beneath.

The automobile was among Macon's first chauffeur-driven cars, and belonged to prominent citizen B. T. Adams, though its owner was not present at the time of the accident. The driver, identified by newspaper reports as "Ira Louther, the negro chauffeur of the Adams automobile," was arrested on the spot.

There was marked disagreement over the chauffeur's fault in the accident. Three young women who were riding in the "tonneau," or open rear seat of the automobile, Mrs. Jennings Adams, Miss Mary Willingham, and Miss Helen Barnes, stated that the driver was not going more than eight miles per hour. But witnesses on the street insisted that Louther "was progressing at a good clip up the hill." The three ladies bolstered their contention by pointing out that the car was stopped over Burge's body and, had the driver been speeding, Burge would have been dragged along the street. The newspaper reported that Louther the chauffer was taken to jail, where he "seemed much frightened by the accident but professed with great vigor that it could not have been helped."

Four hours later, at 9:30 p.m., Charley Burge died at the same hospital where his son would eventually be a patient when his wife was murdered.

Suddenly, Sarah "Sallie" Pullen Burge was a twenty-seven-year-old widow with an eight-year-old son. She was forced to return to work and to depend upon her extended family to take care of little Chester. She managed for a time, and barely a year after she was widowed, Sallie Burge took the necessary steps to manage for a long time to come: She married again and became Mrs. Ben Durden. And Chester's unexceptional life continued well into his teens.

On March 18, 1922, just a few weeks after his eighteenth birthday, Chester was married by Rev. J. D. Ellis to Laurine E. Dupriest whose family was active at Mulberry Street Methodist Church where the Dunlap family was so entrenched. The bride was twenty-three and seemed happy. Later she would say that she had been deceived by young Chester's mother, who told her that her husband-to-be was nineteen at the time of their meeting. Their marriage would prove a particularly disastrous one.

Chester had already begun what he called "investments" (actually petty loan-sharking) while still in his teens and after his marriage continued to operate from home, which his young wife found particularly annoying. Less than two months after their marriage, Laurine moved out. She filed for divorce on August 8, and her petition was officially served on her husband by a deputy sheriff on August 16. The divorce trial, set for November, would prove to be an amazing spectacle.

But first something even more bizarre would happen.

On November 6, 1922, immediately before the divorce trial was to open, Chester's mother petitioned the Court of

Ordinary in Bibb County, Georgia, to lock her son in jail. He was, she said, "a dangerous lunatic," a threat to himself and to others. The record makes no mention of exactly what behavior made Chester dangerous. Her petition needed the signatures of his three nearest adult relatives; thus Mrs. Durden was joined by two of Chester's father's sisters, Mrs. Ollie Wingate and Mrs. John Henderson, as well as Laurine Burge, who was awaiting her trial to divorce Chester. Because there was "no reason being offered to the contrary," the court found Chester to be a lunatic on November 22, and he was committed to the State Insane Asylum at Milledgeville on November 24, just in time for Thanksgiving. There is no indication that he was represented by an attorney or examined by an independent physician. Locked in Milledgeville for almost three months, he was discharged February 21, 1923, and listed as "not insane." There was no hearing to restore his legal competence.

Four months after his discharge, the divorce trial ensued.

Even for a story as textured as Chester Burge's, his divorce trial was unusual. Necessarily delayed until July 16 because of his commitment, a jury was impaneled that included several stalwart citizens among the twelve. Its names testify to Macon's diversity even at that date—DeBorde, Abraham, McGarrah, Farrar. One, Max Lazarus, was the most prosperous jeweler in Macon. His impressive house stood at the corner of Vineville and Pierce, and he was a regular member of the senior Jordan Massee's elite poker group, which was known to play for ruinous stakes. Lazarus's son-in-law would go on to make a fortune with the invention of the Ronson disposable cigarette lighter. For a man who would become so interested in jewelry, it is particularly ironic that Chester's divorce jury would include Macon's best-known jeweler.

What Lazarus and the other jurors heard must have been shocking. For Laurine Dupriest Burge took the stand to testify that although she had been "a kind and affectionate wife," her husband had been cruel. When her attorney, O. C. Hancock, asked in what way her husband had been cruel to her, she answered that he "took advantage of me too many times, four to five times a day." Her answer, evidently, was too subtle, for her attorney then asked, "You mean by that he had sexual intercourse with you?" She answered affirmatively.

"And what was your condition at the time?"

"It made me very nervous and weak," she stated. "It was painful to perform these repeated duties so often."

"And when did he make such demands? At night?"

"Yes. And during the day, when he was working at home."

Laurine was asked if she objected to his advances and answered affirmatively. When questioned whether Chester forced her, she said, "Yes sir, he made me stop ironing to bid to his wishes, he didn't have any regard in the world for what I was doing; if I had a sick headache, he didn't care. He didn't work, he stayed at the house all day." Her attorney asked if she ever told Chester that she did not want to have sex, and she answered, "Yes, one evening I had a headache and told him to let me alone and he said he didn't care."

There wasn't much that Chester's attorney, Judge J. P. Ross, could do under the circumstances. In his cross-examination, he did get Laurine to admit that Chester "was not cruel in any other way." But when he asked whether she was "not physically able to be a wife," she answered, "No woman in the world could stand what I had to go through with." When Ross asked whether Chester had mistreated her in any other way, she replied, "No, he never did hit me. He shook me one night, called me a damn fool, but he never did hit me." Despite this, she was "a nervous wreck ... gone down to nothing." She weighed only eighty-six pounds.

"You couldn't prevent him," Ross asked, "from excessive copulation with you, so you left him?"

"Yes sir."

"You really think you couldn't continue to live with him as his wife without physically wrecking your health?"

"I could not."

After such testimony, Chester did not take the stand.

Laurine's request was granted by the jury—*a vinculo matrimonii*, a total divorce—and Chester was ordered to pay alimony. Laurine retook her maiden name and moved back into her parents' home first at 203 New Street then, finally, at 322 Orange Street. She became very active in the Sunday school program and missionary work of Mulberry Street Methodist Church. She died, before her parents, of a heart attack in the late winter of 1934, after a prolonged illness. She was only thirty-five. Laurine's mother died in 1948 and her father followed six years later. And by that time, Chester Burge was already infamous.

When I uncovered the details of Chester's first marriage, I rushed to Jordan Massee's house to share the news with him. He related a story told to him by the art collector Andrew Lyndon, a friend he shared with Truman Capote. Lyndon was from Macon, and his art collection, including works by Braque and Utrillo, now resides in Macon's Museum of Arts and Sciences. He told Jordan that Lyndon's father, also named Andrew, told him years before that Chester's first wife had a serious curvature of the spine and wore her hair loose to her waist to cover her imperfection. Jordan had not previously related the story to me because, insistent upon veracity, he found it too unbelievable to trust. But his story struck something familiar and I quickly looked through my documents to see what it might be. There, in the newspaper obituary for Laurine Dupriest Burge's mother, Myrtle, was a listing of her pallbearers—included was the name Andrew Lyndon.

———

On April 29, 1924, nine months after his divorce, Chester Burge and Mary E. Kennington were married in Macon by Reverend G. W. Tharpe. If Mary was aware of Chester's prior marriage and commitment to the Insane Asylum at Milledgeville, at least two of her remaining family members were not. As one said, "That's not the kind of thing you'd forget." The couple lived in an area called Lakeside in an unassuming brick house, which still stands at the corner of Morningside and Old Jeffersonville Road.

Mary E. Kennington was from rural Twiggs County, just outside Macon. Her father, Henry F. Kennington, was a farmer and, at one time, a tax collector for Twiggs County. He and his wife, Pauline Mercer Kennington, raised a large family of five sons and five daughters and were active in their Baptist church, moving into east Macon in the early 1930s.

Chester operated a service station and a poultry farm on Jeffersonville Road, where he prospered more from the sale of illegal alcohol than from gasoline. Referred to as "Cackle Hill," his establishment was widely known to provide alcohol during Prohibition, the "Noble Experiment" of 1920–33. He was arrested twice on state prohibition charges. Then, in 1932, he sold liquor to a federal undercover officer and was jailed. He had little choice but to plead guilty to federal charges, and on May 9, 1932, he was sentenced to serve a year and a day in a federal penitentiary.

Imprisonment seemed to have no effect on Chester. In the first year of his release, after Prohibition was repealed and IRS regulations were instituted to govern the sale of liquor, Chester was arrested again in March of 1934 for selling liquor at Cackle Hill without the necessary distilled spirits stamp. He became the first person in central Georgia fined under the new law.

His earlier prison confinement for a year and a day must have been difficult for his young wife. She had given birth to Chester Arthur Burge Jr. on November 13, 1926. His birth was followed the next year by that of a brother. In naming the second son, Chester ignored his own father and grandfather and, instead, chose the name of his great-grandfather, John Lee Burge (the father of Mary, who married Captain Dunlap), for the infant. It was not a clumsy error, as he was already making efforts to ally himself more closely with his wealthy older Dunlap cousins, and his choice of the name of their grandfather, as well as their elder brother who died when he was only seven, could not have escaped anyone's notice.

Then, in 1928, the elder Burge baby, Chester Jr., died after a three-week illness. He was buried in Riverside Cemetery after a service presided over by the pastor of Mulberry Street Methodist Church. Thus, when Chester was sent to prison, Mary was left at home alone with four-year-old John, a position not unlike that of her mother-in-law, who had been left a widow with little Chester to care for alone.

After his release from prison, Chester made a new plan. Liquor alone wasn't the answer, so he began to invest in real estate. But since his commitment to the State Insane Asylum,

Chester had not been restored to legal competence and thus was not legally allowed to own or manage property. The solution was simple: All properties would be purchased in Mary's name.

Always dealing in cash, he purchased slum housing that he then rented to blacks and poor whites. When his business began to flourish, he devised his practice of selling the properties only to illiterate blacks who were most likely to overlook a curious provision called a "retention title contract." It stated that, should a single monthly mortgage payment be missed, the house reverted to Chester and the unfortunate purchaser was not due any reparations for the payments made until the repossession. An eventual lawsuit filed against Chester—actually filed against Mary, as owner—by one of the hapless purchasers claimed that she "continually sells . . . property under contracts similar to the one herein complained of, but that to the best of the petitioners' knowledge and belief, not one person has ever acquired clear title to any property from the defendant [who] allows the prospective purchaser to keep the property for about three years and then bombards the said purchaser with various and sundry legal processes for regaining possession of said realty." The complaint even alleged that the Burges charged extra rent to lessees for the right to use the house's toilet. It became commonplace to drive by Burge properties and see the evicted owner sitting on the sidewalk with every possession stacked on the curb. Bob Steele, the attorney Chester usually employed for his real estate closings, would have Chester sign all the purchase documents and then leave the room. Steele, reportedly in an attempt to soothe his own conscience, would then turn to the purchaser and say, "Now, Chester Burge is a mean son of a bitch. If you miss even one payment, he's going to take your house away. Do you understand?" This was a business with which Chester could support himself and his family. It was not one that would bring Chester the social acceptance he so desperately desired.

So he branched out, opening a nightclub on Jeffersonville Highway named The Eldorado. It was close to Lakeside, a resort area frequented by the young people of Macon.* This era of Chester's life holds one of the very few recounted stories of any kindness, a trait he rarely exhibited, even to his family.

Joe League and his sister grew up on College Street near many of the mansions converted to multiple-family apartment dwellings. Their mother, Ellamae Ellis League, was among the first female Fellows of the American Institute of Architects in Georgia (although she detested being referred to as a female architect) as well as the first president of the Georgia Council of the American Institute of Architects. Joe remembers Chester very well. "There were lots of stories about him all around town about how he wore these spats and hickory-striped pants and the frock coat and the homburg hat—the whole nine yards. He would get on an elevator with people in the First National Bank building and people would just step back and marvel at him because he was so dapper. I think that word was invented for him. That's what he was—dapper."

League remembers Chester's patronage while he worked at the Huckabee auto dealership: "He was a good customer because he bought Cadillacs and he was just mild and meek as a lamb when he would come in there to buy a Cadillac . . . After the War you couldn't just buy one, you had to know

---

* Lakeside would eventually be purchased by record producer Phil Walden, who discovered Otis Redding and made The Allman Brothers icons of the seventies.

somebody . . . He was a good customer. Well, he was very much a social climber. He would buy social position if he could. He had no reluctance at all to do that." That automotive relationship was far in the future, however. At the time Chester owned The Eldorado, Joe League was a bright and talented high school student who happened to draw fine pen-and-ink sketches. Chester saw the drawings and encouraged Joe to create several pictures of young dancing couples. Chester paid cash for all of them, had them framed, and hung them on the walls of his nightclub.

Feeling very important, one night Joe took his date out to The Eldorado where it was easy for an underage high school student to buy drinks. He had carefully counted his money but, when the bill came, found that he was short. Horrified, Joe excused himself from his date, found Chester in the back, and sheepishly shared his situation. Chester slapped him on the back and told him "not to worry about it—it was no problem." The action engendered in young Joe League the only thing I've encountered approaching fondness for Chester Burge, though he readily concedes that, in later life, there was nothing to admire about the man. Says Laura Nelle O'Callaghan, "I never heard anyone say anything nice about Chester." Even when I asked Chester's daughter-in-law if he ever showed her any kindness, she thought carefully and said, "He once told me I had good taste . . . " She paused. "But that was the only nice thing he ever said to me."

As a slumlord and nightclub owner, Chester could only look longingly at the College Street mansions of his Dunlap cousins—to which he was never invited—and dream of taking their places. After Captain Dunlap's death, his widow and their son, young Sam, moved into the grand home on College

Street (sister Ilah had vacated it when she moved to Atlanta's Habersham Road with her second husband, John D. Little). Sam was a worthy successor to his sister, having observed lavish hospitality on his many visits to Europe.

And so Chester watched them from a distance. He watched them with their great mastiffs—ferocious, giant dogs that symbolized their wealth and power. He watched them in their wealth, with their huge white mansions and formal gardens. He watched them with their many servants, with their chauffeur-driven Packard limousine, complete with speaking tube connecting backseat to front. He watched them with their fresh-cut flowers on their doorposts, with the shadowed movement behind the window shades, frequently drawn.

He watched them in their graciousness. As Joe League remembers one of the Dunlap sisters, "Mrs. Wortham gave large sums of money to many worthy causes and to her church. Even in Depression times no one resented her wealth. With the high concrete wall around most of her property, the shades in the limo, and the black lace that she wore most of the time, she had an air of mystery for the children in the neighborhood. But she was *our* mysterious rich lady. Her property was never vandalized, and that large, white inviting wall never once had a word of graffiti on it. Mrs. Wortham's sister, Mrs. Stevens, was also a wealthy widow and lived in a similar house about a block up the street. She also had a chauffeur-driven Packard limousine, even larger than Mrs. Wortham's."

As far from their graces as Chester was, he had a nice view of them. College Street was a study in contrasts: Many of Macon's wealthy families, all in large, single-family houses, were interspersed with the has-beens, those victims of the

Depression, and the young never-have-beens-yet, along with a few working slobs, students, schoolteachers—all but the wealthy renting apartments or divided-up houses.

By watching, Chester knew how quickly a fortune could be lucked into. The Worthams had won a family lottery of sorts. Old Captain Dunlap had told his children that the first one to give him a grandchild and heir would receive $10,000. When the Worthams produced young Samuel Dunlap Wortham in October of 1893, they used the money to enlarge their College Street home by adding a grand front room and pillars across the front veranda. The boy died at nineteen months. There would be no replacement for old Captain Dunlap. After a suitable period of grieving, the Worthams continued entertaining on a grand scale, although Nettie Wortham never returned to church.

One particular evening not long after they had returned to entertaining, the Worthams imported from Savannah a crate of oysters on ice, intending to use them for a dinner party. Wanting to ensure that they had not gone bad in the journey, they fed one to their faithful dog, Bruno, and watched for any negative effect. Seeing none, they readied the dinner and arranged the place cards.

During dessert, while Mr. Wortham was in the middle of a particularly favorite story about Captain Dunlap, the butler entered the dining room solemnly.

"Madame," he announced to Mrs. Wortham, "Bruno has died."

The horrified guests scattered to the bathrooms and the bushes, trying to purge themselves of the fatal course. Telephone calls were quickly placed for ambulances, and faithful family physicians were roused from their own dinners. Only when some sense of order had returned could the butler be heard to say, "Madame, Bruno was run over by a car."

But Chester was never a guest, at that memorable dinner or any others. Try as he might, he could not enter the insular world of his Dunlap cousins. He began to court them assiduously—an approach he must have planned long before, when he gave his son the name of their long-dead brother. But he found their solidarity insurmountable. Over time, though, the cracks emerged, as they died one by one—first young Sam in 1928, Florine Dunlap Starke in 1937, and then the awful year of 1939, which took Lillian Dunlap Stevens in April, Ilah Dunlap Little (the wealthiest of them all) in July, then Nettie Dunlap Wortham in September.* By the time the New Year's bells had rung in 1940, only Clara Dunlap Badgley remained, now alone after the death of her husband during the year that decimated the Dunlap horde. And as the cornerstones of Dunlap crumbled into ash, Chester Burge saw at last his opportunity.

---

* After Nettie's death, a public sale was held to liquidate her personal assets, just as sister Lillian's estate had been sold earlier in the year. Jordan Massee remembered of Ilah, who attended Lillian's sale, "I'll never forget her appearance. She was made up just like Mae Murray in the movies. Bright red hair, tight-fitting black satin dress—almost like a flapper."

CHAPTER THREE

Even late into the decade of the 1930s, the wealthy American visitor considered Germany a necessary stopping point on the grand European tour. The country's soothing mineral waters were thought to be so beneficial that a self-indulgent visit to London and Paris could be atoned for by a slightly ascetic visit to the baths. The traveler was denied few creature comforts, yet he or she could proclaim self-denial even if such protestations bore little relation to reality. Among such amenities, Adolf Hitler was hardly thought of by an American visitor, and if he was, it was most likely as that man with a funny mustache whom Charlie Chaplin so cleverly imitated.

Of course the American visitor had seen spread across every newspaper at home the photographs of Hitler at the 1936 Olympics, where Jesse Owens, a black man reared in Alabama, humiliated the Führer's image of a superior Aryan race by winning four gold medals. Though the atrocities against Jews, Gypsies, homosexuals, and others had already begun subtly in Germany, the overwhelming view of America's upper class was that those troubles did not concern us. Why boycott Germany when its internal problems weren't our affair?

For the wealthiest Americans, like the Dunlap sisters, travel to and from the country was unencumbered. Their friend Jordan Massee Jr., who was often in Germany from 1936 through 1938, clearly remembered that Germany was extremely receptive and hospitable to American tourists because of the money they brought into the country. It was only after *Anschluss*, the

March 11–13, 1938, invasion of Austria, that the American government began to dissuade its citizens from traveling to Germany, and Massee and others like him ended such visits.

The Dunlap sisters had long included Germany on their annual European sojourn, and the U.S. government's warnings had no effect upon them. Their correspondence was full of references to extended foreign trips. As early as May of 1928, Nettie Dunlap Wortham wrote of an impending "stay of six months in Europe," and those visits continued throughout the next decade. And even after *Kristallnacht*, the Night of the Broken Glass, when more than two hundred synagogues were destroyed and 7,500 Jewish businesses burned, the American visits continued. It was the custom of Ilah Dunlap Little, the wealthiest of her family, to take the waters in Baden-Baden each year, and she had no intention of letting Germany's internal political troubles change her itinerary. In the summer of 1939, Mrs. Little went to Paris with a paid female companion, as was her custom, then on to Karlsbad. There she died unexpectedly on July 26.

It was shaping up to be an unfortunate year for the Dunlaps, as Clara Dunlap Badgley's husband had died in January, followed by Lillian Dunlap Stevens in April. With Ilah's death in July, only sisters Nettie and Clara were left. While the American consul in Dresden, Germany, cabled (collect) for arrangements to have Ilah's body returned,* her family was notified that her jewels, said at the time to be worth $200,000

---

* To R. C. Dunlap, Chevrolet Motor Co., Macon, GA. "I regret to state consulate at Dresden, Germany, reports unfortunate death Ilah Little. Following telegram from Consulate: Quote your twenty-first. Court Commissioner cabling and writing you. Says he may need about one hundred sixty dollars from you to settle local claims as he cannot cash Little's express checks. Consulate doing everything to expedite matters."

(though some rumors went as high as a million dollars), were too valuable to entrust to a courier, and they would only be turned over in person to a family member. Nettie Dunlap Wortham was in rapidly declining health and would in fact follow Ilah in death only seven weeks later. Neither Nettie nor Clara could possibly make the trip. As word spread of the predicament, Chester Burge sprang into action.

He began with violets. It was Clara's favorite flower, he had somehow learned. After enough of them, she finally decided there must be something good in him despite what her sisters thought and said. So she received him. As Chester was the only family member available, he likely seemed to Clara and to Ilah's executors the only option to retrieve Ilah's jewels from Germany. In the late summer of 1939, Chester Burge was finally—if begrudgingly—accepted into the Dunlap family fold and was dispatched on an errand to Germany. His trip must have taken place very soon after Ilah's death, because on September 1, 1939, 1.8 million German troops invaded Poland and World War II began. Only thirty-five, Chester was safe from the impending draft, as his 1922 adjudication as legally incompetent had never been reversed. His country still thought him crazy.

And after his return from Germany, more than a few other people did as well.

His story was this: On his way back to Macon, Chester decided to take the jewels to Tiffany's in New York City for cleaning. When he did, Tiffany's said they were only worth a few thousand dollars for the platinum and settings; the diamonds were all paste.

Macon was then divided. Either Chester Burge had stolen the Dunlap diamonds, or the Nazis had. Or neither. As some claimed, including Jordan Masse, Ilah never did have any fine jewelry. She could have afforded them many times over if she had wanted, but she preferred the costume jewelry in which she decked herself.

An obscure Georgia legal case (*Orient Insurance Company v. Dunlap et al.,* 193 Ga. 241, 1941) partially supports this theory. After Ilah's death, a German court commissioner valued one of the necklaces in her possession at $60,000. But when the necklace arrived in the United States, it was found to be "of Japanese or cultured pearls" and worth only about $60. Ilah's executors had paid insurance premiums amounting to $2,775.42 on the necklace and sued the Orient Insurance Company for a refund of $2,430, alleging a mutual mistake as to the character and value of the necklace. In an October 1941 ruling, the Georgia Supreme Court barred the executors' recovery, holding that the insurance company carried out its contractual duties and, had the necklace not been safely delivered, the company would have been liable for the entire $60,000 valuation. In reporting the decision, the *Atlanta Constitution* referred to the story of "a necklace which bests even de Maupassant's favorite imaginings."

But the case also presents a compelling argument that, for once, perhaps Chester Burge was falsely accused. Ilah's executors were led by Robert C. Dunlap, who, though not a family relation, became intimately involved in their business affairs and acted in the same role for several of her sisters.* He employed American Express, through the American Con-

---

* His son, in writing to his own daughters in 1970 of R. C. Dunlap's responsibilities, included this paragraph: "Chester Burge of Macon was a notorious, degenerate, and lawless individual. His grandfather's sister was Mary Burge, wife of Captain Sam Dunlap. Chester Burge's history was almost unbelievable, and I won't go into all the lewd and lurid details."

sul in Dresden, to have Ilah's personal effects shipped from Germany. They were dispatched onboard the steamship *Manhattan* on June 11, 1940, almost a year after her death. R. C. Dunlap was present when the package was opened in the New York City offices of the Guaranty Trust Company. It was then discovered that the necklace, which had been valued in Germany at more than $60,000, was actually valued at $61.50. There is no mention of Chester Burge as having had any part in the transaction, and his name appears nowhere in the legal case.

Whether or not Chester proved himself by traveling to Germany, it is certain that he began to draw his net more tightly around seventy-year-old Clara. Ilah's will had left a trust fund of $750,000 for the erection of a memorial library at the University of Georgia. She even specified that the building be of red brick and encircled with columns. But first her two surviving sisters were to enjoy the income from the estate for their lives. Upon Nettie's death only weeks after Ilah, the income was to be paid solely to Clara. Ilah's home on Habersham Road in Atlanta was to be sold, as well as her large estate, Oakland, in rural Lee County, Georgia. With Ilah's financial assistance, Clara had her own plantation, "Listenin' Hill," near "Oakland." According to one attendee at Clara's parties, "She loved beautiful things. There were beautiful things in that house that were absolutely of museum quality. There were some gorgeous things."

Nettie had been so ill that she was unable to attend the funeral of her sister, Ilah. In fact, during her last two years her affairs were governed by bank guardians as she had been declared "imbecile from age and illness and incapable of managing her own estate." When she died at her home in

Charlottesville, Virginia, on September 13, 1939, Clara was with her. Nettie's substantial fortune left $200,000 each to Wesleyan College's endowment fund and to Macon's Mulberry Methodist Church, and Wesleyan's trustees promptly renamed a dormitory in her honor. The college president announced that "this bequest will repair the breach in our endowment fund caused by the Depression and will put us in much sounder position." The portraits of her parents were to be hung at the church, where they still reside.

Clara was then left all alone, her substantial fortune a tempting target for Chester. After winning her confidence, he began to cut her off from all those around her. When she would complain that her old friends had stopped calling, Chester only replied that he was her family and friend and that should be sufficient. Soon, Clara's health began a serious decline. The doctors seemed unable to understand what was wrong with her. Chester's response was to voice his distrust in the "hick town" physicians frequently enough to convince her to go to Johns Hopkins.

"Well, how would I ever get there?" she asked.

And he said, "My wife and I will take you in our station wagon."

The story, prevailing and still extant in Macon, is that Chester placed a mattress in the back of his car for Clara's comfort while he and Mary drove her to Baltimore. The trip was also to include a visit to Clara's properties in Middleburg, New York, and a brief stopover at Camp Peary, Virginia, to see Mary and Chester's only child, John, then in naval training. The next day, August 18, 1944, Clara supposedly asked Mary Burge to write a new will for her. A copy of the result still exists in Mary's meticulous handwriting, leaving a few special bequests, but the bulk of her estate, valued at more than a half million dollars in negotiable stocks alone, was to go entirely to John L. Burge, whom she had first met only the day before. Clara's signature was purportedly executed and witnessed "at a filling station" once they reached Baltimore.

According to Chester's subsequent testimony, Clara "dropped her will in a mail box" at the Windsor Hotel in New York City. On that same trip, Clara refused to stay in a particular New York hotel because her dog, Peggy, would not be allowed to remain in Clara's room. "Peggy was not going into the basement with common dogs," Chester later testified. Clara's "Baltimore will" even specified that Peggy's body eventually be embalmed and placed in the Dunlaps' vault in Macon's Rose Hill Cemetery.

Why would the new will benefit Chester's son and not Chester? Other than the fact that Chester still had not regained his legal competency, it appears that Clara had a stronger determination than he imagined. Her 1939 will, written when she first became the only remaining Dunlap, left a few small bequests to friends and her late husband's relations, while the bulk of the estate was to benefit orphanages in Macon, in Dougherty and Lee Counties (where her plantation was located), and in Middleburg, New York, where she had lived with her husband.

In June of 1944, in response to Chester's tightening grip on her, she amended that 1939 will so that her rural plantation, "Listenin' Hill," was left to Chester's son, "whose name, I understand, is John Lee Burge" (she had not even met him at that point). But that amended will also carried a strongly worded last provision stating that, should Chester or Mary Burge contest it, the bequest to their son would be void.

Evidently the August 1944 will, effected while on their trip north, was still not enough for Chester. Perhaps he became concerned that a legal challenge to it might be successful. For, in January of 1945, Chester and Mary visited Clara at her plantation and brought with them a newly typed will for her signature. After making the usual small requests to friends and servants, this last will gives "all my jewelry, my Buick automobile, all of my furs, linens, silverware, and all other household furniture" to Mary Burge. An additional $1,000 bequest was left to Mary to care for Clara's beloved dog, Peggy. "All of the rest and residue of my estate of every kind and character, including real property, personal property, or mixed property" was left to Mary Burge in trust for the benefit of her son, John, until he reached the age of thirty-five. All the family portraits went to Mary, while Clara's trusts for the benefit of orphanages in two states were suggested in this last will although their establishment was to be "entirely discretionary with the said John L. Burge." Catherine V. Eckstrom (perhaps a nursing assistant hired by Chester) was the only witness to the handwritten Baltimore will other than Chester and Mary, and she again witnessed this later one. Clara's shaky signature, dated 11 January 1945, whether real or fake, was to be her death warrant. Three days later she died at Chester's home.

Chester's social ambition led him to Macon's fashionable Shirley Hills, where one resident who lived nearby remembers, "He thought we all dressed for dinner." He first purchased what is now the Hartman home at 1173 Oakcliff Road, complete with a garage apartment (formerly servants' quarters), to which one neighbor recalls a nightly procession of cars driving down the alley to obtain illegal whiskey from Chester, who apparently hadn't fully given up the old profession. As former neighbor Laura Nelle O'Callaghan recalls, "Everybody had a fit when he bought" the house on Oakcliff.

The Burges were not received with open arms. Already infamous as a bootlegger and former prisoner, Chester was an upstart crow at his very best, and, as O'Callaghan recalled, "just trash" at his worst. One matron ordered her daughter not to speak to them, as the Burges' handsome son caused concern for those families with teenage daughters. Considering Chester's emerging proclivities, perhaps the greater worry should have been for those families with teenage sons. But that would come to light in time.

Chester's burning ambition for social acceptance led him to befriend several widowed matrons in Macon. Evidently the path to social acceptance did not have to lead through the front door. He was eager to offer his chauffeur-driven car for their afternoon enjoyment, and some finally relented in their loneliness. Mrs. Charles Schaefer, who was the undisputed social doyenne of East Macon, frequently accepted his invitation to Sunday afternoon rides around town with her wheelchair in the trunk for those occasions when she wished to pay a personal call.

Laura Nelle O'Callaghan, who then lived three doors from Chester, had never met nor spoken with him at the time, but she remembered the following from January 14, 1945:

My mother had had a stroke but she could get up and everything. We had a real good black woman who had been with us forever. One Sunday afternoon I came in and she said, "Miss Laura, Mr. Burge called and he wants to take Mrs. Anderson [her mother] to ride with Mrs. Badgley this afternoon." I said "Well, I don't know about that," and she said, "Well, I told him I'd have you call him." I decided no and I called down there and he answered in this terrified voice and said, "I can't talk to you now, I can't talk to you now!" All of a sudden he hung up. That was the afternoon she [Mrs. Badgley] died. There was some question about whether he killed her. He had never called Mother to ride before and I wondered if that was going to be his alibi. There was a lot of chitchat about it at the time.

Supposedly Mrs. Badgley had been ordered, for medical reasons, not to drink alcohol, but strong rumors still persist that she had several martinis at Chester's house on the afternoon she died. As one contemporary recalls, "Chester kept her liquored up." Jack Caldwell remembers rumors that Chester may have smothered Clara with a pillow. There was no autopsy.

She was the final Dunlap to take her place in the family vault. If her dog Peggy was later interred with her, as she wished, there is no record of it.

An estate of Clara's size was big news in 1945. Her negotiable stocks and bonds alone were valued at more than $512,000, while her itemized appraisal of silver exceeded three single-spaced legal pages. Her jewelry and furs took another two pages, and her three cars (including the Packard touring sedan) were placed in storage awaiting the outcome of the disposal of her estate. Even the contents of the hand-bag she was carrying at her death—"4 old fountain pens, 1 hair ornament, 1 letter opener, 1 pr. glasses and case"—were appraised as having "no value."

The resulting legal challenge to Clara's will was among the most important trials ever held in Macon to that date. The University of Georgia was to be a substantial beneficiary of Ilah's estate after her sister Clara enjoyed the income from it for her lifetime. The university promptly hired the prominent Atlanta law firm of Powell, Goldstein where Ilah's second husband had been a partner. The remaining beneficiaries, including the interests of the various orphanages, retained the Macon law firm of Jones, Jones & Sparks. They argued that both the handwritten "Baltimore" will and the final "Albany" will should be thrown out in favor of Clara's original "Atlanta" one.

Early in the challenge process, the arguments for the handwritten Baltimore will were assumed to be so weak that the process centered upon the Albany one written three days before her death. The battery of expensive attorneys argued that it was not Mrs. Badgley's signature or, alternatively, if it were, she was not competent to sign and had been coerced or tricked into doing so.

They argued that Clara "was weakened by mental and physical disease and old age" and that Chester had set out to "ingratiate himself into the good graces" of his cousin. They alleged that Clara successfully resisted his efforts to make gifts of property to him, then finally relented to some degree by including his wife in the will. At the trial it was disclosed that, on June 2, 1941, Clara changed her will by leaving "Listenin' Hill" to John Burge and that, owing to Chester's persistence, she signed over the property to John in a deed of gift dated June 23, 1941.

But, according to their allegations, that was not enough for Chester. He attempted to have Clara place him in charge of her financial and legal affairs, but she refused "because she knew that he was a person of bad character and reputation . . ." He became so persistent, they alleged, that "after June 1944, as the result of his continued pressure she finally got to the point where her will was entirely subservient to his will, and where she was in her weakened conditions unable to resist his overtures and importunities."

Chester's efforts to control her life, it was claimed, extended to his preventing her "from having persons such as the minister, her intimate friends, and others, to call upon her and to visit her, except in his presence, and often refused to let them into her house even when he was there, and for some reason did not wish them to see her. He endeavored always to be present when anyone having a right to see her for business or other reasons came to see her. He undertook to handle her business affairs. She had a physician of her own selection, but he undertook to furnish her with medical attention of his own selection. He browbeat her and intimidated her in the selection of nurses and paid companions, in the selection of specialists, and in respect to her coming and going. It got to the point where she was unable to refuse to do anything that he directed her to do."

Still, after all this, they alleged, Clara would not sign the will leaving everything to him and his family. According to their allegations, Chester and his wife drove to Clara's Albany plantation on January 11, 1945, "and had her sign a paper which he represented to be a claim under an insurance policy for a burglary loss, and had it witnessed by three witnesses not in her presence . . . She signed this will under trickery just three days before she died."

Chester wasn't about to lie down. Represented by the Macon law firm of Hall & Bloch, he was joined in his petition by his father's sisters, including Mary Burge Henderson, who had co-signed him into the lunatic asylum at Milledgeville more than twenty-three years previously. On the opposing side were the several modest beneficiaries of Clara's original will, with one curious defector. Martha M. Badgley of New York City, a relation of Clara's late husband, was left $10,000 in the handwritten Baltimore will and, in the contested "final" Albany will, her bequest was reduced to $5,000. She joined forces with the Burges in attempting to have either of those accepted as Clara's final wishes.

In April of 1945, attorneys representing the original 1939 Atlanta will presented their case to the Bibb County Ordinary Court presided over by Judge Walter C. Stevens. Fully expecting overflow crowds, officials moved the hearing to City Court chambers. The first legal bombshell took place in May when Mary Beacom of Atlanta, a handwriting expert often retained by the FBI, testified that Clara's signature on the Baltimore will had been traced and was not original. Not to be outdone, Burge's attorneys aced their opponents by presenting as their witness Albert D. Osborn, the handwriting expert whose testimony helped convict Bruno Hauptmann in the Lindbergh baby kidnapping case. He testified that Clara's signature was genuine and valid.

The battle had begun.

To dispute the accusation of his greed and the charge that Clara had been under his control, Chester took the stand. He testified that he remained by Clara's bedside for five weeks when she was seriously ill. He said that Clara remained at his home because "no Dunlap had ever been to a hospital." He asserted to the court that "Clara was perfectly capable of taking care of her own affairs" and cited several instances in both her business and personal life when she had exercised her own independence. One was her ordering that only "pressed turkey" could be served to her beloved dog, Peggy, when Clara traveled to New York with the Burges. He insisted that the New York trip was her own idea as she wanted to retrieve some furniture from her former home in Middleburg.

The trial was recessed until June, when Chester's attorneys could present their case. During the recess they filed for a continuance, arguing that John Burge, the chief beneficiary of the proffered wills, was in U.S. Naval service in New Hampshire and could not be present in court. Under the law then in effect, cases affecting the interests of soldiers and sailors must be postponed indefinitely until the person could appear in person or waive his presence. The law was valid for sixty days after discharge and was not affected by leaves or furloughs. Opposing counsel argued that the motion should have been filed at the beginning of the hearing and was thus offered too late for consideration. While waiting for a decision from the judge, Chester's attorneys presented the testimony of Mrs. E. C. Eckstrom of Washington, who testified that she witnessed the contested will and that Clara was "in her right mind" when she signed it. Judge Stevens then denied a continuance and the hearing drew to a close in late June after two final weeks of testimony.

Rumors in Macon continued to circulate as the jury took the conflicting evidence under consideration. Burge's case was considered flimsy by many, but the testimony of his famous handwriting expert could not be discounted. Not until December was a decision finally reached. Before Judge Stevens even announced a verdict, both sides declared their intention to appeal. After consultations, the judge called the jury into the courtroom and directed them to reach a verdict in favor of the original Atlanta will. The competing parties had reached an out-of-court settlement in favor of the Atlanta will but with an undisclosed amount to be given to John Burge from the estate as a result of the directed verdict. The judge publicly announced that he believed the settlement to be the best result for both parties.

The settlement, never made public, gave John Burge full legal possession of Clara's large rural plantation, "Listenin' Hill," complete with family portraits, etc., as well as the sum of $105,000. His mother was awarded clear title to jewelry and furs given to her by Clara during her lifetime. Martha Badgley was given $5,000 and the other beneficiaries had their bequests reduced proportionately to enable the payments to the contesting parties. The University of Georgia could proceed with the construction of the Ilah Dunlap Little Memorial Library, although its encircling columns were, by financial necessity, confined to the front façade while the remaining three sides presented fake columns built into the brick. Even today, a fund of more than $860,000 exists in a Macon bank in Clara's name for the benefit of local orphanages, while more than $880,000 of her funds remain in an Albany bank to benefit orphanages in that area.

In September of 1947, Mary Burge signed a receipt acknowledging that she had collected all the evidence in the files of the Court of Ordinary in the Badgley case, including the original Baltimore and Albany wills. As John was under-age at the time of the settlement, both the plantation* and the money were under his mother's legal guardianship. To Chester, this represented a mere technicality. Now armed with cash and a base for entertaining, complete with antiques and ancestors, he was ready to begin his social ascent.

---

* "Listenin' Hill" was eventually burned to the ground with all its treasures in what was widely suspected to be insurance fraud.

CHAPTER FOUR

"I had heard so much about Chester Burge that I imagined him with Polly Peachtree patent leather hair, a pigeon gray silk suit, and a pearl stickpin in his tie. I was never so disappointed in my life when I finally met him," says Mary Sheridan, whose father, Otis Knight, one of the most literate men ever to live in Macon, was among the few to befriend Chester and Mary's son, young John, when they took up residence on Oakcliff Road. By all accounts, John was as pleasant as he was handsome, but he was never able to escape the onus of being Chester's son. Although "Listenin' Hill" was owned in John's name, he left the use of it to his parents while he pursued his studies to be a college professor. His 1949 engagement to Caroline Elizabeth Cook was particularly important to Chester, since she was a girl from exactly the kind of family to which he aspired.

Soon after the engagement announcement, Jordan Massee's father ran into Chester Burge downtown, and offered him a "fine seventeenth-century Venetian mirror I think would be just the sort of thing for you to buy for your son's forthcoming wedding." Chester agreed to come and see it. With John in tow, Chester waltzed into the Massee home. John took one look at the mirror, knowing his plans to move with his wife into a bungalow, and said charmingly, "Well, it's a whole lot taller than our ceilings are going to be, I'm afraid." It was clear that Chester had planned the outing simply to get a view of the Massee home, to engage in his favorite pastime of critique and comparison, and to gloat over the Massees' recent loss of their fortune and home. While John stepped outside and talked with the elder Massee, Chester came back inside where young Jordan and his two sisters were down on their knees wrapping up china and putting it in barrels.

Chester said, "You children were born with gold spoons in your mouth, and now you can't even afford to hire some blacks to pack up your china."

Young Jordan didn't stop his work but said softly, without looking up, "Chester, what we were born with we cannot lose and you cannot buy."

John needed to chart a different course. And he aimed to do so. Caroline Cook, called "Cookie" by her friends, taught at Wesleyan College's fine arts campus, called the Conservatory, on College Street in downtown Macon. A daughter of Mr. and Mrs. Walter Scott Cook of Charleroi, Pennsylvania, she had attended New York University and graduated from Carnegie Institute of Technology. Though she was slightly older than most of the fraternity members and not a student, she was elected Mercer University's Kappa Sigma fraternity sweetheart for 1948–49, which speaks well of her attraction and charm. Her future husband, John, was a member during that year, having become a student at Mercer upon his graduation from Augusta Military Academy after attending both the Georgia Military Academy and the University of Havana in Cuba. Cookie must have seemed to him both an attractive lover and a fresh start.

The couple had a traditional wedding on June 12, 1949, at St. Paul's Episcopal Church in Macon, which greatly pleased the groom's parents, who paid for the expensive honeymoon. After the wedding Mary and Chester left immediately for a four-month trip to Europe, where they were to visit the families of two Spanish civil war refugees, Manuel Alvarez and Basil Tariche, who had been frequent guests of the senior Burges when they were classmates of John at the Augusta Military Academy. The *Macon Telegraph* proclaimed that, during their absence, the senior Burges were "turning their Shirley Hills home over to the young couple." After the honeymoon, the young couple's planned-for bungalow never materialized, for they moved in with his parents. The bride was expected to stay at home, help her mother-in-law with cooking and cleaning, and to abandon her life and the friends she had made. The house immediately became her prison.

A prominent attorney in Macon had been close friends with Cookie before her marriage. When John proposed to her, she came to see her friend to ask his advice. She said that she loved John but was worried about his strange family. The attorney could plainly see that she was in love and told her to follow her heart. After she returned from the honeymoon, she called him and, in whispered tones, said that she was being held in virtual captivity and that she was not allowed to leave the Burge home or to make any calls to her friends. She rang off quickly when someone entered the room.

Not long afterward, the same attorney received a frantic call from Cookie, this time not from the Burge home but from a nearby town. She told him that she had surreptitiously placed a call to her own mother, whom she instructed to drive down from Pittsburgh and to be in her car outside the Burge home at an appointed time. Cookie was able to run out the door holding only the clothes and possessions she could carry in one mad dash. They drove away quickly, and once they were clear of Macon, she placed a call to her friend to thank him and to let him know what she had done.

There was to be no reconciliation. The groom waited eleven months then filed for divorce, claiming he had "performed the duties of a faithful and affectionate husband," but that, upon their return from the honeymoon, his wife treated him "in a cruel and inhumane manner." John insisted that Caroline "abused and reviled" him, along with his "mother and father and was guilty of ungovernable outbursts of temper." Finally, he claimed to have "provided her with a comfortable home and all the necessities of life and such of the luxuries as he was able to afford but, nonetheless, her dissatisfaction grew continually worse until, without any reason or excuse and after abusing and vilifying [him]," she returned to her parents' home in Pittsburgh. Caroline did not contest the divorce in any way and asked only for $1,000 to pay her attorney fees, for which she gave up all financial rights and privileges. And she immediately retook her maiden name. She wanted nothing more to do with the Burges. Chester's grandson, John Lee Burge, remembers that Neil Diamond's song "Sweet Caroline" always brought a smile to his father's lips, which invariably annoyed the boy's mother, the elder John's second wife.

According to one source close to the family, John was "heartbroken" when Cookie left him, so Chester had to find a suitable wife for his son. If an arranged marriage was good enough for the youngest Dunlap daughter, then surely it was good enough for John. Chester must have thought that was how things were properly done. He had left matters up to John the first time, and it had all fallen apart.

The Burges' friends, Anna and Peter Olesen, had a pretty granddaughter named Anne Gerin. She had just finished high school at Georgetown Visitation, a proper Catholic girls' school in Washington, DC, founded in 1799. At the urging of John's parents, the Olesens showed him Anne's graduation photo, and he was interested enough that Chester, Mary, and John planned a visit to the Olesens' home in Minnesota. Anne took the train from Washington to Minnesota to join her grandparents before beginning junior college in the fall. The three Burges, Anne, and her grandparents drove up to the north country, where they stayed at what Anne remembers as "a lovely lodge." On the way they stopped at a service station where they saw a bear chained to a post. Chester decided he must have it to put in a cage in his backyard with his peacocks, so "he bought it, had it crated up, and shipped home." The act greatly displeased Anne, who decided that "Chester was a spoiled brat and his son inherited that trait."

Before Anne left on the train to return to school, Chester and Mary showed her their family jewels and gave her two bracelets of diamonds and sapphires. She says she "wasn't blown away but did feel sort of like Christ being tempted by the devil in the desert." They tried to talk her into accepting the idea that John would be a good husband and provider for her. As Anne now says, "Money had always been an issue for our family but it didn't trump morals." They implied to her that, at the very least, she would have her education paid for by John. "I liked him as a person. He was a handsome guy and on his best behavior," she remembers. But she had no intention of being talked into something as foolish as marriage. Fortunately, John made no mention of an immediate wedding, and Anne thought they could get to know one another by correspondence over the coming months. Before she boarded her train they convinced her to take the two bracelets, and she wore them on the train to Washington. Evidently the Burges viewed them as the equivalent of an engagement ring.

John later came up to Arlington, Virginia, to visit Anne's family for a few days although he did not stay with the Gerins. Anne's brother remembers playing bridge with him during the visit. Her mother, in the meantime, found out that John was divorced and that the marriage had not been annulled, and she was concerned that Anne was going to be convinced to marry him. As Anne's brother says, "Divorce in our family was *verboten*." Their mother even called a nun at Anne's school to ask her to talk Anne out of any thoughts of marriage. Anne says now, "I can't imagine why she thought I would have gone through with it. They didn't even ask me if I wanted to marry him. Back then kids were not supposed to ask questions or contradict adults."

Anne was a freshman in junior college when she walked out of class one afternoon, shocked to see Mary Burge waiting for her. The three Burges had been driven up in their limousine, and Mary said to Anne, "We're going to take you home." Naturally Anne assumed she meant her home in Virginia where her mother would be waiting for her. When Anne got into the limousine, she was introduced to their attorney, who was in the backseat with Chester and Mary. She got up front with John and the driver. Once they were on their way, Chester said to her, "We're going to pick up your grandmother at Union Station." Anne became increasingly concerned about what was happening. She knew it wasn't like her grandmother to show up unannounced. When they stopped to let John go into a hotel to retrieve his baggage, "I got really scared and decided I was going to get out of the door on the passenger side where John had just been sitting. Chester saw what I was about to do and got out and sat in the front seat by the door so I couldn't get out," recalls Anne. Her grandmother, Anna Dickie Olesen, arrived at the train station and climbed into the backseat with Chester, Mary, and the family attorney. Then, says Anne, "We turned onto the Richmond Highway and I got really scared because I knew we weren't going to my home." Anne thought very seriously about jumping out of the moving car even though she knew she might be hurt or even killed. The Burges had told her mother they were in town and were driving Anne home, but they did not tell her that Anna, the grand matriarch, was arriving. "We stopped for dinner at a nice hotel in Richmond where they called my mother," says Anne. They told her that Anne was safe. They also told her "that John and I had been married." The elder Anna was put on the phone to reassure her daughter that everything was all right. Then, Anne says, "I started pretending to go along with it and told them to tell my mother that I would just go down to see everything in Macon then return to school."

The group spent the night in a motel along the way. Anne and her grandmother shared a room, and the next morning Anna told Anne that John had sat outside the door of the room all night long so she wouldn't leave. "She thought it was so romantic," says Anne. In the privacy of their room, Anne was able to tell her grandmother that this was all a terrible mistake and "she started coming to her senses."

The group got to Macon, and Anne was given Mary's room. In fact, she slept in the same bed where Mary's body was found when she was murdered. Chester showed Anne "all the crystal and china and antiques and let me know that, if I married John, all this would be mine and I would be mistress of all this." She was also told "we would go and get blood tests the next day" in preparation for the marriage.

What Anne didn't know is that her mother had convinced the boyfriend of Anne's sister to drive her to Richmond to try to find the group. She wasn't successful, but learned there was a waiting period to get married and they had lied to her. It was obvious they were headed to Macon. She called the police, but they told her Anne was eighteen and legally an adult, so there was nothing they could do to intervene. Anne's father was a Navy captain away at sea, leaving his wife to rear three teenagers alone. There was very little money and she certainly didn't have enough to buy an airplane ticket to Macon. So she sold the family car immediately to get the cash. She arrived in Macon early the next morning and took a taxi to the local Catholic church. She had to find where the Burges lived, and that was the only thing she could think to do. After learning the address, she went to her parents' home and picked up her mother, Anna.

Back at the Burge home, Anne rose from bed and went into the bathroom, where she "began praying my head off. I prayed to the archangel Michael to come rescue me." Mary went down to breakfast, and Anne decided to wait a few minutes. Then, perhaps she could sneak out the front door. When she got to the landing on the stairs, there was her grandmother. After riding in the taxi with her daughter, she had walked up to the front door of the house. As was normal in Macon at the time, it wasn't locked. She walked in the door and up the stairs and ran right into her granddaughter.

Anne didn't know her mother was outside in a taxi, but her grandmother said to her, "Run! Run and I'll stay here and face the music." Anne did as she was told, jumped into the taxi with her mother, and they drove off immediately. She sent the bracelets back but she never saw the Burges again. She says now that the only good thing that came out of that experience was an abiding friendship with a priest at Georgetown who helped her deal with the ordeal afterward. Even after all these years, she is amazed that she was kidnapped, but even more astounded that the Burges and her grandmother could have thought she would go along with their plan for an arranged marriage to John.

To a man of Chester's social aspirations, the house on the hill at the corner of Nottingham Drive and Jackson Springs Road must have seemed a halcyon idyll. The city's social and power elite lived on those two streets in tasteful and under-stated comfort. As one contemporary said of him, he was "an ambitious redneck" and there could have been no better home in which to launch his social ascent than that of W. T. Anderson, publisher of the *Macon Telegraph*.* When Chester purchased the house, he moved barely one block, but it was far more suited to his needs.

Joe League recalls of the house, "There was some crystal and china and silver in it when he bought it. It wasn't his. I don't mean that he stole it, he probably paid for it—but it had other people's monogram on it and there were other people's portraits in the house, and he just adopted them as his because that gave him social position, he thought." Chester began entertaining on a grand scale even if old Macon stayed away in droves.

Try as hard as he might, Chester could not attract the "A-level" guest list he so desperately craved. One old Maconite of distinguished lineage recalls, "They had big

* Charlie Nash owned the house after Anderson and sold it to Burge.

parties, but we never went—my grandfather would turn over in his grave!"

Joe League, however, was obligated to attend. "Well, nobody wanted to go to his parties; they didn't want to get that close to him. But people were obligated for business reasons, like the law firm that represented him, the banks that he did business with, and the people he bought Cadillacs from."

In fact, Burge expected a great deal for his patronage of Huckabee Cadillac. As League recalls, "When he would bring his car in for service, normally they would offer to send someone to take him home, or Mary could come pick him up. But, no, he didn't want to do that. He would get me to take him home because I lived out here [Shirley Hills] so that was an excuse. 'Why can't I just go home with you?' Well, there was hardly any way I could get out of it because he knew I was coming out here and it was time for me to come home and he had engineered that. But I wasn't gonna get out of that car and come in his house with him and I never did. But that's what he wanted me to do." Burge would be insistent: "All these times he would almost get down on his knees and beg me to come in the house and have a glass of wine or something." When it came time for the big Christmas party, however, League had no choice.

"Well, this one time I had to go. I sort of lost the drawing of the straws so I was elected. So Mary Jane [his wife] and I reluctantly went to the party. We decided we would go and put in an appearance, and if we're there more than five minutes we'll be gone and we will have done our duty. Well, the minute you get there you are escorted into a room—a living room, a music room, a study, and a dining room—and all of them had sliding pocket doors. Well, we were ushered into a room and the doors closed behind us and we couldn't get out. Chester would say, 'You'll be interested in talking to these people,' like they did in the military . . . We had a terrible time getting out of there and finally they escorted you into a room that had the food. It wasn't bad but all this stuff in the house was not his. I mean, he owned it because he had bought it, but it wasn't his originally. It was somebody else's social position."

But all that entertaining took money. Chester always dealt in cash, and more than one contemporary recalls stacks of money in the house. Hal Anderson, who was to become a friend of John and his second wife, insisted that "Chester used to take John with him to collect money in the red-light district close to Camp Wheeler, and there would be much, much cash in shoe boxes."

Gerald Mullis began practicing law in Macon in 1951 and quickly became familiar with Chester's business practices since "he had acquired and owned probably more of those substandard houses than anyone else in Macon. When I started practice, he was already the owner of the largest number of black homes—generally shotgun houses that, under today's laws, would be condemned. If he found someone who was going to be able to save their house, he would check for any small claim against them then he would buy that claim and use it to commence foreclosure by tacking it onto his note. Same thing with ad valorem taxes. He would pay unpaid taxes, even if they were up to date, on the mortgage. He would tack it on and use it to foreclose. He would do that only on those who were getting close to paying off their mortgage."

Obviously Chester's business practices endeared him neither to his clients nor to those who were aware of his duplicity.

Mullis remembers, "All his black clients were in controversy against him. I saw him and his wife in court on at least one occasion. He was a very hostile type of litigant. I'm afraid to describe him as I felt at the time." As a young attorney just entering practice, however, there was very little Mullis could do to bring Chester to public account for his deeds. "After I had a chance to see how he was doing those black people and seeing them in foreclosure . . . I started clipping notices out and mailing them to the owner of record with a letter, but nowhere did my name or address appear. Unless you studied the ads you'd never know your house would be sold on the courthouse steps. In that day there was no requirement of notice. He'd run that ad one day a week for four weeks then buy it back and foreclose on them. My letter told them they needed to see their attorney. His lawyer came to me and threatened to report me to the State Board of Ethics. I said, 'Go ahead!' . . . I think a lot of those black people were able to save their houses."

Rex Elder, formerly president of Macon City Council, was Chester's neighborhood grocer, and because of his intimacy with city officials, he knew a great deal about Chester's business affairs. Elder confirms Gerald Mullis's story of corrupt real estate practices. "When a purchaser had been good and kept up all their payments, if they were about to pay off the note, Chester would say to them, 'You've been a good client—buy a nice present for your wife—just don't pay this month.' Then he'd move in and foreclose."

After his disastrous first marriage, Chester's son John was more fortunate. His second wife was "a real nice girl," as former neighbor Laura Nelle O'Callaghan remembered. She was Jo-Lynn Scott, daughter of Leita Robertson Scott and O. V.

Scott Sr. Jo-Lynn and John were married in 1952. Fritz Phillips, whose entry into the family circle would eventually contribute to its downfall, says of the young bride, "I thought Jo-Lynn had something wrong with her because why would she marry into that strange family? Her parents were first rate. I don't think they particularly liked Chester Burge one bit."

Two children were born to Jo-Lynn and John: John Lee Jr. (called by both names) in 1953, and Mary-Leita, who was named for her two grandmothers, in 1958. John Lee was born with a serious medical problem (usually described as stomach-related) that required expensive medical treatment. His grandfather Chester agreed to pay for the expenses if little John Lee came to live with him and Mary. John Lee's birth parents became known to him during early childhood only from their infrequent visits. Chester's mother, Sarah Durden, whose second husband had died by then, moved in with Mary and Chester to help care for the little boy.

Chester grew very fond of little John Lee, but their closeness evidently turned Jo-Lynn against her own son. Several sources insist that she openly disliked the boy. One who was to become very acquainted with John recalls that little John Lee "had gone off to camp and came back with his suitcase and hadn't used any of the clothes. She flew into a rage and yelled, 'He's just like Chester!'" Another friend "tried to get her to send him off to boarding school to get him away from her, but she didn't." The boy seemed to be genuinely loved by his father, and John Lee "appeared to do anything to please his daddy." But, another insists of John and his son, "John would have him shoot a squirrel in a tree then make him skin it right there. The boy seemed to be so vulnerable and just wanted to get his father's approval." Hal Anderson agrees, "John Lee had a very hard life as a child, and we all felt so sorry for him because Jo-Lynn, for some reason, apparently despised the child. She never missed an opportunity to embarrass him. Why I don't know. The rumor was that when he was born he had a physical defect. Chester said he would pay to have it corrected but only if they turned the child over to him." Fritz Phillips also agrees: "I never really thought that Jo-Lynn thought much of him, that is, since he was the product of Mr. Burge and not a Mercer-Scott type of person," referring to Jo-Lynn's own family.

Mary-Leita received the love and attention their mother denied John Lee while their father appeared to love them both. Mary-Leita was born with epilepsy, and at one point, when she was faced with a serious illness, John visited his closest friend, Dr. Leonard Campbell, and cried as he related his concerns for the girl's well-being.

Little John Lee became part of Chester's household. Now that he had his family, his home, and possessions, of which he was inordinately proud, it was time to turn to his own wants and needs. He had given Mary jewels, furs, extended trips to Europe, and a certain social standing. They had a son of whom they were justly proud and two grandchildren, one of whom lived with them. But what about Chester's own desires? Wasn't it finally his turn?

As Joe League asked me, "You know what Chester was, don't you? Chester got caught in the Lanier Hotel in the men's room soliciting and trying to pick up people. He was bad and everybody knew it." When I asked whether Chester had been arrested for it, League answered, "Not exactly. The police got him, but he talked or bought his way out of it. But he was that bad—picking up people in men's rooms."

There is no doubt that Mary would have known of Chester's activities. In fact, her later actions seemed to have condoned it. But, as Jordan Massee surmised, "She probably thought that what Chester did in business was no different from what other businessmen did. But carrying on with the boys, that was entirely a different thing. If he did that in New Jersey, at least nobody in Macon knew about it. But doing it here was another matter."

Chester eventually was to solve the problem by addressing it "in-house," although it was a crooked path that led him to the solution. As befitting his rank, he expected to have servants in his home. And, as a babysitter for little John Lee recalls, "The chauffeur and maid always wore a uniform with hat." At one point, Chester hired an immigrant Jewish couple from Frankfurt, Germany, where he traveled to interview them. They were part of the U. S. government's efforts to repatriate displaced persons after World War II. They were told they would be given a monthly salary of $140 plus a furnished apartment including all utilities. They were also promised that the latter of the two to survive would be given $10,000 cash so long as they stayed in Chester's employ. Upon the couple's arrival, they were taken to the law firm of Chester's personal attorney, William Turpin, of the fashionable and prominent firm of Turpin and Lane. There they signed a contract witnessed by Peter Olesen, Anne's grandfather, who was a professor of German at Mercer University (and a name that would figure prominently in Chester's future).

They were also taken to Atlanta to be outfitted with uniforms at Rich's department store. But they were unhappy almost from their first day and complained of their treatment by Chester. They wanted to buy an automobile, but Chester had not given them any of their wages, insisting that he had yet to be repaid for their uniforms. He then agreed to buy a car for them, but when they quit after ten months and demanded the car, they learned that he had purchased it in his own name. Chester complained of the experience when the President's Commission on Immigration and Naturalization held hearings on the repatriation of displaced persons in Atlanta on October 17, 1952.

Mr. Turpin's representation of Chester was a puzzle to folks in Macon. One young attorney for the firm, fresh out of law school, remembers that Mr. Turpin "seemed to value Chester as a client and I, along with other people, wondered why . . . Mr. Turpin was a great lawyer, dignified, courtly, beautifully mannered, and the very picture of what a fine lawyer at the pinnacle of his career should look like."

One incident concerning Chester early in the attorney's experience with the firm remains very clear in his memory even though it happened in the fall of 1949, just after he graduated from law school. "I was on the elevator one day in the Bankers Building to go up to the office. There was a colored man on the elevator along with Mr. and Mrs. Burge. I do not recall the order in which we got on the elevator, but I recall that the colored man kept on his hat, which displeased Mr. Burge enormously. He flew into a rage. He berated the man mercilessly to the extent that, to a bystander and onlooker such as I, it was embarrassing and irritating. Chester so overdid it that I undoubtedly would have said something to him or maybe even gotten in a fight with him except that I knew that he was Mr. Turpin's client, and I couldn't afford to offend one of his clients. So I held my peace. The man absorbed the verbal blows very gracefully and humbly, and the vitriolic attack on him by Chester went without response. It was such an unwarranted attack, and so acerbic in its tone, volume, and rudeness, that I have always remembered it though it has now been over fifty years ago since the incident happened." When asked how the object of this tirade reacted, the attorney responded, "While the unfortunate man was in no social position to respond, I admired him for being such a gentleman about a totally unwarranted verbal attack. If he left his hat on in the elevator, as I believe he did, this certainly did not warrant the vituperative and vitriolic attack which Chester launched at him in my presence."

There is a popular and verified story concerning Chester and his friendship with Mr. Turpin. Valuing their relationship, Chester wanted to give a substantial gift to Mr. Turpin as evidence of his appreciation for being represented by such a respected attorney. The Turpins lived in a lovely stucco home at the corner of Hines Terrace and Ingleside Drive. They had painted it a shade of pink and waited several years for it to weather and fade into the exact hue they were seeking. Mr. and Mrs. Turpin left for an extended trip to Europe and returned to find that Chester had, in their absence, arranged to have their house painted green as a surprise gift. The current owner, Ed Sell III, uncovered the paint during a subsequent remodeling. When Ed was just a boy, he and his family lived on Laurel Avenue in a neighborhood that abutted Shirley Hills but could not match its social cachet. The Burges kept large and noisy peacocks in their backyard, and Sell clearly recalls seeing Chester being driven down Laurel Avenue by his chauffeur in a large black Cadillac searching for his escaped peacocks.

By this point Chester had begun hiring only blacks as his house servants. The first chauffeur, Eugene "Gene" Robinson, was a parolee. He drove for Chester for several years and also ran errands for the Burges. Rex Elder, who owned the neighborhood grocery where Chester shopped and kept a monthly tab, remembers receiving a call on the day before the Burges were to give a big Thanksgiving party. "Chester called us in that high-pitched voice and asked, 'Where's the food?' I told him we were really busy and he sent Gene down right away with the station wagon to see if he could help us."

Although Gene would continue working for the Burges, his days as Chester's chauffeur were numbered once Louis Roosevelt Johnson entered the scene. Gus Kaufman was head of G. Bernd & Company, an animal feed processing business founded by his grandfather. He clearly remembered Louis Roosevelt Johnson, who came to work for him briefly at G. Bernd & Company. "He was so flamboyant. He wore big rings and he spoke very intelligently and seemed educated. He had lots of phoniness. I don't think we took that much notice of him until we later found out he was involved with Chester Burge. We didn't really check their backgrounds then." Had he checked, he would have learned that Johnson had been sentenced to fourteen to twenty years in prison in Michigan in 1948 for having killed a woman he was "courting" (sometimes referred to as his wife) by hitting her on the head with a stick, causing a wound from which she died two days later. He was released in July of 1957 from Michigan State Prison and was still on parole for second-degree murder.

Johnson stood out in Kaufman's memory because he was "effeminate and flashy. I remember being amazed that he would come down to our place and do common labor. It was hard labor and kind of smelly. We were good employers and treated people with dignity. Rather than pay them enough, we treated them with dignity." Kaufman's own mother had a full-time chauffeur who lived in and was paid $2.50 a week. Even for those low wages, it was easier work than manual labor in a hot and smelly animal processing plant.

Johnson was recommended to Chester by his parole officer, Don Walters, and was hired later in 1957. Chester definitely could use a man with Louis' skills. And, of course, there were the side benefits to consider.

CHAPTER FIVE

Frederick Morris "Fritz" Phillips Jr. was exactly what Chester Burge wished to be—a product of the finest schools, the culmination of distinguished bloodlines, and at ease in elegant social settings. But there was an important difference between the two. For Fritz, these were not learned or purchased behaviors. He was born to them.

After coming across Fritz's name in my research and locating him in New Jersey, I wrote an obsequious letter of introduction, telling him that I knew it must be difficult for him to recall such distasteful memories as Mary Burge's murder and the notoriety that was thrust upon him as the young object of Chester's physical attractions. I was more than surprised, then, on my first call to learn that he was not only eager to talk about it but also had absolutely no reservations about describing events exactly as they happened. In fact, he seemed to relish relating sexual details. During that first call, however, he told me that I must only speak to him before lunch because he started drinking then and nothing that he said under the influence of alcohol could be believed. Within a few years, however, he stopped drinking and smoking for medical reasons and welcomed my calls at any time. But there was one inviolable rule—he would not see me. No matter how often I offered to visit and interview him in person, he insisted that he was "old, fat, and toothless" and didn't want me to see him this way. It was an image that was incongruous with the role he played in Chester's saga.

As our cheery emails progressed (his always ending, "Keep Smiling"), Fritz, who is a divorced father and grandfather,

began attaching innocent but suggestive photos of bodybuild-
ers from the 1950s in "posing straps." Later, the attachments
would cross the line into full nude shots until I remonstrated
and asked him to stop sending them. He contritely apologized
and ceased until he "forgot," and the process would start all
over again. He is particularly fond of the sexually suggestive
drawings of Tom of Finland, most especially when the sub-
jects are in various stages of shedding military or police uniforms.

Fritz lives on a thirty-four-acre family estate in a historic
home built in 1741 and remodeled in 1942 by his parents. As
he says of his present life, "My sexual orientation is no secret
but, living in a tiny town for so long, I guess that I am thought
of as the funny old fat queer. Well, I am that funny old fat
queer." And on another occasion he insisted, "My weight has
gotten to humongous proportions because I no longer smoke
or drink. All I do is think about sex and make off-color jokes
to the workmen who work on the house. We all make an effort
to improve the property and to enjoy each day the best we
can, with a smile." Mobility has also become a concern for
him "for the past eight years, since I had a disappointing hip
replacement as the result of a fall when my dog knocked me
down and broke my hip on the frozen ground. The dog was
destroyed and I now stay here in my house."

Fritz's background was as close to blue-blood as Chester
Burge could ever hope to acquire. As he glibly told me early
in our conversations, "My family built the *Monitor* that beat
your *Merrimac* . . . My grandmother was from Mount Holly and
her uncle ran for governor but was defeated by his classmate,
Woodrow Wilson." When Fritz eventually married, his family
connections grew even more impressive. "My wife's Bedford

family is an old colonial one and seem to be prominent in the generations after the Revolutionary War. They migrated across North Jersey as judges and lawyers and then to Wilkes-Barre, Pennsylvania. There they connected with the wealthy Reynolds family (descended from the *Mayflower*) and prospered." The Bedfords, like Fritz's family, were Princeton graduates and benefactors. Fritz attended prep school at Blair Academy and the William Penn Charter School before volunteering for the Navy in the Korean War. After four years at sea, he entered Princeton (where his father was a 1923 graduate) then studied hotel administration at Cornell (where his grandfather was an 1879 graduate). Unlike some of Chester's pretensions (late in life he insisted his family name should be pronounced "Burjay"), all Fritz's claims to a distinguished lineage are verified. His family has figured prominently in the Social Register for decades, and several of their homes are listed on the National Register of Historic Places. Even the writer Edith Wharton, the most acclaimed chronicler of life in the strict regimes of upper class New York society, was a cousin—born Edith Newbold Jones.

Fritz's introduction to Chester Burge took place through the intervention of a family member. "My great-aunt, Mae Shreve Hutchinson, went around buying up mortgages. She and her husband, Newbold, my great-uncle, would travel around Georgia in a trailer—no one in my family would have dreamed of doing that on the East Coast. She just got meaner and meaner, but she made money at it. We called her Aunt Mae. She and Chester were sort of friends. Chester and Mary were beguiled by my sister, Lydia, who was exactly John's age. John was invited up here to some dances. He was very good-looking but frightfully shy. Lydia then went down to Macon but came back early after John tried to put the moves on her. Aunt Mae left millions to the Presbyterian Church and some to Uncle New. We inherited our education through him . . . he set up trust funds for all of us to get our college tuition paid for so even with me, it amounted to my share of about $250,000, and that ain't hay."

It was through Mae and Newbold Hutchinson that Chester first met Fritz at their New Jersey estate, Medowby, in 1958. "The first time that I laid eyes on Mr. and Mrs. Burge was when they invited my beloved sister to Macon as a date for John Burge to take to a dance. The idea was that she was a suitable Northern young lady and more could probably transpire. It didn't. She thought that the whole lot of them were strange; she didn't like them and came home." Mae had died by this time, and Fritz was helping his aged uncle Newbold by driving him when he needed assistance.

"I am only guessing but maybe Uncle New had asked Gram [Fritz's grandmother] to entertain them [the Burges] for cocktails or something and maybe that's when the thought of my driving them to Georgia came up. I strongly doubt that Chester had asked Uncle New whether or not he had any nephews who would drive them south and give him blow jobs at the same time.

"Somehow I wound up spending the night over at Medowby, perhaps to get the early start. I don't know, but I don't think that we stayed the night anywhere along the way. We did eat at truck stops and the like because, I learned, both Mr. and Mrs. Burge drove bootleg liquor down from Canada and so knew all of the routes and cheap stops for food. Uncle New had cautioned me that I was to spend *nothing* because Mr. Burge had agreed to pay for all expenses, and so we drove straight through, getting into Macon late at night. I was polite and cheerful as a professional driver would be when an old uncle had asked for a favor.

"I also recall that I was given the room to the left across from the master suite. Mrs. Burge was sweet and what you might expect from a Southern lady. But Mr. Burge was doing his best to be boorish and carp about *everything*. He had had an operation or some such thing, and so I put it off to that, but Mrs. Burge seemed to think that everything was normal, I guess. She was quite pretty and, as was shown me several times, she wore a very large diamond ring, which Mr. Burge was repeatedly telling me that he had given to her. I didn't think that it was odd that he would give his wife a large ring, but I questioned the appropriateness of wearing a thing like that for every day. After that I think we called a cab the next morning and I went to the airport and back north."

But Fritz was far from finished with the Burges as Chester was obviously smitten. He started inviting Fritz to fly down for his grand parties, and other invitations resulted. As Fritz now says, "I guess Chester thought he would just fly me down whenever he got horny, but that got to be boring, too." There were some benefits for Fritz, however. He was able to travel and be entertained at Chester's expense, and there was also the occasional introduction to someone who interested him. Macon's then-wealthiest resident was P. L. Hay, who founded in 1904 the Bankers Health and Life Insurance Company. By 1937 the business had more than $25 million of policies in effect just in Georgia. In 1926 Hay had purchased Macon's grandest residence, the Johnston-Felton House, where the remaining Confederate gold was rumored to have been hidden when the retreating Confederate cabinet had its last meeting before disbanding in flight.*

P. L. Hay was also among attorney William Turpin's prominent clients. As word of Chester's extravagances began to surface, Mr. Hay went to see Mr. Turpin, delivering an ultimatum that Turpin could represent Banker's Life and Mr. Hay or he could represent Chester. The Burges soon found other representation, although Turpin did deign to serve as one of Mary Burge's pallbearers.

Hay's son, P. L. Hay Jr., was vice president of his father's company and lived next door to Chester on Nottingham Drive, although Fritz remembers that Mr. Hay Jr. "was about to sell his house to get away from Chester." The Hays had a very handsome and talented son, P. L. Hay III, whom Chester could not have failed to notice. Only months after Mary Burge's murder, young P. L. entered the recording industry. Credited as "Wanderobo," he released on the RCA record label a single, "Voice of the Wind," that some thought might have been a hit with better promotion (in an atypical uncharitable quip, Jordan Massee called the single "more wind than voice"). The Anita Kerr singers provided background vocals. Another single was "That's What Girls Are For," cowritten by Phil Spector.† At one point the handsome young actor Tab Hunter came to Macon to visit Hay.

---

* President Jefferson Davis was captured at Irwinville, almost one hundred miles below Macon, on May 9, 1865. He grabbed his wife's raglan, or raincoat, and threw it over his shoulders as he fled his captors. That action led to the persistent but totally erroneous rumor that he was trying to escape dressed in women's clothes.

† Spector was the originator of the "wall of sound" production technique and a pioneer of the 1960s "girl groups." He produced the Academy Award–winning Beatles album, *Let It Be*. Spector was charged with the 2003 shooting death at his home of actress Lana Clarkson and, after a 2007 mistrial, was convicted in 2009 and sentenced to nineteen years to life.

Joe League was very active at the Macon Little Theatre, where young P. L. Hay III began to volunteer. Says League, "He was gay. When I found out, hanging around the Little Theatre, I didn't like that. That changes your opinion. He was a handsome boy." Fritz concurs, remembering him with particular fondness. "P. L. Hay, the father, went to school with my wife's father, Hugh Bedford, at Princeton Prep." He remembers young P. L. as "the cutest little thing—just adorable. He was a 'pin-up boy' with lots of muscles and dark curly hair. I guess I wasn't his type 'cause nothing ever happened. He took me to meet his grandmother in that huge house where she lived—it was just exquisite." Of the visit, Fritz relates, "I do recall going to the Johnston-Felton-Hay House to meet the grandmother. She was very sweet to me, much to my surprise. I recall that P. L. showed me where the treasure of the Confederacy was hidden under the staircase, and he also very proudly showed me how the statue at the end of the ballroom would be allowed to turn. The house was simply beautiful although really a museum and not a home at all. At any rate I loved seeing it."

After the Burge murder took place, the police found young P. L.'s name in Chester's little black book. The Hay family used its considerable influence to ensure that the fact was never made public, and the boy was not questioned. He later moved to Hawaii, where he assembled an extensive beachfront estate, PollyMakena. When we spoke and corresponded in 2003, he professed to have only vague recollections of Chester, Fritz, and the murder. But, in a subsequent conversation, a few details came to mind. He lived in the apartment behind his family's main house and remembered going over to visit the Burges once. The only things that stood out in his memory were the parrot, which he remembered as living in the kitchen, and Mary's "beautiful ring." He was certain, however, that the Burges "were never accepted by the elite" in Macon. Hay is now deceased.

Fritz's visits to the South began extending beyond Macon. On one occasion, "We went shooting at the Santee Club in South Carolina—those teeny-weeny quail that you in the South evidently don't feed. I didn't like shooting, but I liked the idea that gentlemen do it, so I went shooting." He saw enough of our foibles and our eccentricities that he "thought how awfully funny you people in the South are." When he told me, "Chester's cousin was a fat lady in the Florida fair. There were lots of strange people who worked at the circus," I decided that he surely was exaggerating. But Chester's grandson, John Lee Burge, recalls his "aunt" the fat lady. According to him, she was so enormous that "she had to turn sideways and squeeze to get through a door." Because she could not climb the stairs, during her annual visit through town the Burges would make a bed for her on the ground floor. Little John Lee received welcoming hugs from her that he recalls almost smothered him "between her big tits."

The fat lady was Frances Hope Voges, called "Baby Frances," weighing in at 826 pounds. She was certified as the fattest woman in the world by the *Guinness Book of World Records,* which called her "the closest approach yet to the spherical woman." She had a 73-inch waist and 64-inch calves. Baby Frances traveled with the circus from Canada to the West Indies and even made a circus trip along the coast of Africa. In the first grade she weighed 190 pounds and, at the age of fourteen, gained five pounds a week on a strict diet of water and lettuce. During a twenty-four-hour fast, with a doctor by her side the entire time, she gained two pounds. When Baby Frances first joined the traveling "fat show" in 1953, she weighed 560 pounds. She drove a specially equipped Cadillac with two sets of shocks and a double frame and flew only on Eastern Airlines, as they knew her exact weight and always calculated where in the airplane to seat her to achieve maximum balance. Because she could not climb the stairs, she was placed onboard with a hydraulic lift. Frances's divorce from her first husband was granted as she sat in her car on the curb in front of the courthouse because she could not fit in the building's door. When Baby Frances died in 1978, she was buried near her 402-pound daughter, Darlene, who toured the circus with her mother. Darlene had been a normal-size teenager until she had a double bout of pneumonia as a teenager and quickly gained 250 pounds. Baby Frances's Tampa newspaper obituary was titled REQUIEM FOR A HEAVYWEIGHT. A cemetery worker waiting to lower her into the ground was quoted as saying, "That's a big casket, but death is bigger than all of us."

The Burges and their extended family were, indeed, a strange group. According to Fritz, of the entire Burge family, "None of them fit into any society I've ever known." His family agreed. On one of the trips that young John Burge made to New Jersey, he stayed with Fritz's grandmother. "She thought that he was different because he went to bed with a bottle of bourbon, and that seemed odd to her."

The Burges had joined Christ Episcopal Church in 1957. On a social level, it was even a step up from Mulberry Street Methodist Church where the Dunlaps had long worshipped. According to one longtime member, "People turned and looked when they came walking in." Evidently Chester was trying to widen his circle of friends. Buck Melton, who would later become one of Macon's most successful mayors but was city attorney at the time of Mary's murder, recalls of Chester during that period, "He wanted to be seen and associated with the topflight people in town."

One of Mary's nephews, Leon Kennington, remembers his aunt Mary as "very regal." Leon drove a moonshine truck for Chester before entering college, but his uncle Jake, Mary Burge's brother, warned him not to find himself alone with Chester because he might be sexually propositioned. Leon recalls "key parties" at Chester's house where couples would throw their car keys into a pile. "Whichever key you picked up was who you went home with." When asked about the incongruity of such a practice while Chester was becoming more sexually active with men, Leon answered, "I guess Chester did that so everyone would think he was straight."

When Fritz would come down for big parties at the Burge home, John and his wife, Jo-Lynn, were frequently guests as well. Although Fritz was having sexual relations with the father, it was the son whom he eyed lasciviously. When asked whether he accompanied Chester to any equestrian events near Anderson, South Carolina, where Burge liked to visit, Fritz responded, "I have no recollection at all of horses except for John's purported size and reported stamina."

Fritz never had the opportunity he desired, but he was close enough to hear of John's sexual prowess. John arranged a hunting trip for Fritz that he remembers clearly. "I didn't like hunting at all, but I was trapped . . . The guide got pissed off at me because I wasn't interested in shooting at all, and he pointed out that I was a lousy guest because John had gone to a lot of trouble on my account and that I didn't appreciate it."

But it was on the trip back that things progressed in a grotesque way. "On the way back to Macon from the quail reserve, we stopped for what I was informed was the usual celebratory drink after the hunt. So we all three went into the roadhouse where the activity was rowdy and fun. John disappeared and got laid and after he had shot his wad upstairs, we all left and finished driving back to Macon with the guide fucking the bitch dog and telling me how much better his lay with the dog had been compared to what John had gotten with the girl; and what's more, that probably wasn't all that he had gotten." Fritz remembers his embarrassment when the girl described John's sexual prowess to them all. He wistfully recalls, "Every once in a while there would be a slim chance that Jo-Lynn would be absent and then I would have been able to bunk with John, but it never happened."

Sleeping arrangements at the Burge home seem to have been unusual as well. Fritz remembers, "I was never offered the garage quarters because John and Jo-Lynn were almost always there. Louis [the chauffeur] was even berthed in Chester's bedroom on the floor so that I would sleep in the master bed." With the master. Not surprisingly, Chester and Mary had separate bedrooms. His was larger and, according to Frank Lanneau's daughter, Marie, who babysat little John Lee, "Chester had a big high four-poster bed with drapery around the tops and sides—like something you'd find in Europe. John Lee was on Chester's bed a lot when being tube-fed." The Lanneau family visited John Lee there in Chester's bedroom occasionally. Marie also recalls that, "Chester always wore a silk smoking jacket or fancy silk robe. He always talked to us." Another exotic furnishing Marie recalled was downstairs. "In the living room there was a yellow silk chaise lounge where she [Mary] read in the afternoons. It had drapery above it. There was also a large beautiful portrait of Mary downstairs with a light shining on it. Marie's younger sister, Kay, was John Lee's age and became his playmate. Marie and Kay both remember John Lee and his grandmother fondly. Marie also recalls that, while the Burges "had big parties, John Lee and I had a cold bowl of split pea soup and some crackers in the pantry and stayed in the pool house with the children while they had all this great food at their parties." Marie also remembers his baby sister, Mary-Leita, in a crib and that she "was given a baby bottle to feed her with that night in the pool house." It wasn't just the food, either, that Marie found cold. "Jo-Lynn did not seem to be a warm person. She was rushing to get dressed for the party. She gave me instructions about keeping John Lee and the baby in the crib. His grandmother [Mary] loved him."

Fritz remembers very few of his experiences with the Burges fondly. "Once while I was staying there at the Macon house and waiting for the Christmas party, I persuaded Mary and Jo-Lynn to take a walk with me. We went down to the river and it was clear that it was a unique experience. At that time both ladies were warm and soft and vulnerable. It was a departure from the usual implacable roles that they played."

But such moments were rare. Fritz asked and answered his own question, "What role did Mrs. Mary Burge play in the family tableau? At first, she was the pretty wife of an eccentric, strange Southerner but after a while, she also evolved as herself strange. When all is said and done, she was equally complicit because she was bound to the money and the house. She was treated shabbily by both father and son though at the same time she was respected, seemingly, by both. The relationships were complicated because, like in *Cat On a Hot Tin Roof,* there was affection and revulsion at the same time. Generally speaking, Mary Burge allowed a great deal of leeway to both men. Chester in his gangster behavior and the son's philandering and drinking. She seemed to gain her importance for the very reason that she allowed the two men to rage on unchecked. They tromped on her sensibilities and cherished her at the same time."

Fritz also thought it an exceedingly strange household with a chauffeur/butler (Louis), a handyman (Gene), and a maid, Jessie Mae Holland, who were all parolees. "I thought it was so odd to be locked up in a house with a murderer, Louis, and the laundress who had also been in prison. The laundress seemed to understand the setup and, of course, never challenged it. I had been led to believe that she had killed a man, perhaps her husband, with her own bare hands. It was a colorful household. She must have known about Louis and I imagine even got him to fuck her from time to time."

Even though Chester obviously desired to have the absent Fritz with him as often as possible, some of his needs were more immediate. Tommy Bush, who was then a student at Lanier High School, worked at his father's service station and tire store downtown. He was a handsome boy and immediately attracted Chester's attention during the summer between his junior and senior years. He remembers Chester as "an overly attentive, overly charming man when he came in to have his Cadillac filled with gas. He seemed overly interested in me. I could recognize lust in somebody's eyes."

Chester asked Tommy if he would like to accompany him to Europe the following summer. Tommy decided that it "might be a good idea and maybe the only way I would ever get to Europe. My family wasn't wealthy. We were working folks to live with the rich people." Tommy knew there would be trade-offs for such an opportunity. "I wasn't totally dumb . . . I could tell from the way Mr. Burge looked at me there was going to be a price to pay to go to Europe, but at that point I wasn't totally opposed to paying it. He wasn't *that* unattractive."

Of course Chester would need permission from Tommy's parents to take him to Europe. He remembers, "It seemed months later when the subject came up. Mr. Burge came to our house at night. He said that all my expenses would be paid plus I would receive $500 spending money. There was a written itinerary. My father shook on it. My mother wasn't real happy. He was at our house about forty-five minutes." The trip was scheduled for the summer of 1960. Tommy then entered his senior year at Lanier "and began to read about Europe."

Jordan Massee had heard this story but didn't know the identity of the young man, inaccurately referring to him only as "a mill village boy," which denoted that his family had limited financial resources. As he told his version of the story, Chester "met this boy from the mill village and started wanting him and lavishing gifts on him." According to Massee, "Mrs. Burge had had enough of Chester's foolishness. That's when she went to the mother of the mill village boy. The parents just couldn't praise her husband enough for being so kind and generous to their son. They were so pleased that Chester was taking their son to Europe to look after things for him— they assumed that's what rich people did. So Mrs. Burge said, 'You don't understand,' and told them the real reason Chester was taking their son. Well, they put a stop to that right away and told their son never to see Chester Burge again."

Joe League was a neighbor of the Bush family and confirms the story. "Tommy was gonna go to Europe for six weeks with Chester Burge . . . Chester even told me about it. He just casually told me about taking somebody, but I don't know that he ever even told me who it was. But he was gonna take somebody with him, like some big benefactor or something, he was gonna take him on this wonderful trip. Well, Mary Burge heard about it and she called Arlene [Tommy's mother] and she said, 'Arlene, don't let him go,' and told her why. Well, Arlene didn't know that about him. She didn't know Chester at all except that he was somebody who lived in a big house and had a lot of money, but didn't really know anything about him. So Arlene stopped him, she didn't let Tommy go." When Chester's mother, Sarah Durden, testified at his trial for Mary's murder, she said she heard a discussion involving a young man in Macon who was to accompany Chester on a trip until Mary objected. Durden said of Mary, "She thought it was wrong to take the boy off."

Tommy was never aware of the real reason his trip was cancelled. When I told him those stories almost fifty years after it happened, tears came to his eyes and he said softly of his mother, "She *did* love me." It was an affirmation he needed. He now remembers of the entire incident, "It shook me to my foundations. I often wonder what my life would have been like if I had gone. I began flunking Spanish. Nellie Lamar was my favorite teacher and she took a great interest in me. When everything [about his planned trip with Chester] became public, I became like a germ at high school. Everyone avoided me. I tumbled from my pedestal from the social elite to an untouchable. It just crushed me. It was like I had the plague but I found out I did have friends. My parents even sent me to a psychiatrist. I overcame the stigma, but it was very upsetting. Much later I ran into Chester in the Trailways men's room."

Joe League directly attributes Mary Burge's death to her interference with the planned trip. "That's when Chester became furious with Mary and had her killed," he insists. Jordan Massee agrees, "That's when Chester decided that Mrs. Burge was not an asset, she was a liability." As the Burges' family veterinarian, Dr. Herman Westmoreland, remembered, Chester "decided he was just going to put her out of her misery and go on and do what he wanted to do." But things weren't a complete loss. There was still Fritz to accompany Chester to Europe.

CHAPTER SIX

Chester's hilltop house was particularly well suited for land-scaping. The property sloped gently down toward Jackson Springs Park across the street, and during winter it was some-times even possible to gaze through the defoliated trees and see the Ocmulgee River with Rose Hill Cemetery on the other side. The Dunlaps all rested in permanent splendor in their impressive mausoleum at Rose Hill, with Chester's own Burge grandparents not far away. Long before it was the Burges', the home's lawn had originally been beautifully landscaped but, remembers Laura Nelle O'Callaghan, "When my uncle [W. T. Anderson] lived there they just let it go because it was during the War. Then Mr. Charlie Nash bought the house. They cut down so many beautiful pine trees and everyone just had a fit. Chester was trying to cover it all with camellias." Some even contend that the chauffeur, Louis, removed camellias from Jackson Springs Park under cover of darkness and replanted them in Chester's yard.

Thom Phillips worked as a teenager at his family's nurs-ery, Phillips' Garden Mart. He remembers Chester's "arro-gance" whenever he would come in to buy camellias. "It was like an event when he would show up as he was a bit bigger than life. He was a big spender and money was not a factor." When Chester would choose which of several shrubs to buy, he would spend an unusual amount of time going through every one before making a selection, as Phillips remembers. "He wouldn't even sign a ticket for the bill because he must have thought it was beneath him. But he did pay his bills in full and on time." When Phillips would help load the purchases into the car, he remembers that Chester "would insist that lots of newspapers be placed in the trunk so there would be no dirt or water to stain the inside of his Cadillac." What he remembers even more clearly, however, is the interaction between Chester and his chauffeur, Louis. "The body language between the two was just not right. They were much more like husband and wife, or at least best friends. There was no indication of a servant-master relationship, and Louis never acted like a chauffeur by opening Chester's door or deferring to him in any way. It was obvious that Chester put up with a lot of insubordination from him."

Jack Caldwell was present when one of Chester's attorneys asked him about his relationship with Louis. Chester declared simply, "I love that nigger." There is no disputing the fact that Chester and Louis had sexual relations in the house, often with Chester's mother and Mary at home. As one who was intimately acquainted with matters insists, Louis had his own room and bath in the basement, and Chester "would openly tell the chauffeur to wash up and come upstairs." There they would lock the door with orders not to be disturbed.

Fritz believes that, far from being coerced into the relationship as Louis later claimed, he actually enjoyed it. "He really had it good in his situation. In a way, I think that he really liked having sex with the master. It gave him a small reassurance that he was worthwhile. He frequently slept at the foot of the master's bed because Mary slept in another bedroom. Actually, I would have liked to have had a threesome, but at the time I didn't know how without getting jealous and leaving someone out." Fritz was quite aware that Louis had little reason to welcome him to the household. "How he must have hated me, but then again perhaps he was happy to have the old ogre distracted for a while."

What Mary thought about all this is not certain. She rarely ventured out because, as Laura Nelle O'Callaghan recalled, "Mrs. Burge was not social . . . I saw her one afternoon at the local grocery store shortly before she was killed." Rex Elder, who owned the neighborhood grocery, remembers, "Mary was a cold person; I never heard her laugh. I never saw anybody in my store speak to Mary. She was a serious-type person. She wore jewelry all over; it was so pronounced."

Even with Louis close at hand, Chester's plans always included Fritz. At the time, Fritz had begun working as an assistant manager at a newly opened Sheraton Hotel in Philadelphia. Chester decided that he would find a hotel in Florida for Fritz to run and the two could live there happily together. Fritz remembers, "Chester and I went on a two-week toot to Florida and spent our nights together in bed, which was *boring*." But, given the prospect of running his own hotel barely out of school, Fritz was amenable. "Chester offered to buy me a hotel somewhere near St. Petersburg, Florida. All he wanted to do was get in my pants, which I let him do 'cause I thought it was part of the job." Of course, the only problem was the need for a large infusion of cash to buy the hotel. And, since Chester had been declared mentally and legally incompetent between 1922 and 1956, all the many income-producing properties purchased during that time had been placed in Mary's name, and Chester did not have legal access to them. Even the Burges' home on Nottingham Drive was owned solely in Mary's name.

By this time Fritz had become a serious issue in the family. As likeable as he was, it was obvious this was no ordinary fling for Chester. As Jordan Massee reasoned, "carrying on with the boys, that was entirely a different thing. If he [Chester] did that in New Jersey, at least nobody in Macon knew about it. But doing it here was another matter."

At the end of the two-week trip Chester and Fritz took in January of 1960 to look for a suitable hotel in Florida, the two visited Chester's mother's cousins, Olivia and Edwin G. Kyle, at their home in Tampa. Olivia was the sister of "Baby Frances," Frances Hope Voges, the fattest woman in the world. Chester told Olivia that he was "in love" with Fritz and intended to leave Mary for him. He also explained that he would need access to the capital he shared with Mary in order to buy their hotel.

Mary arrived to join the group in Tampa, accompanied by Louis, the chauffeur, and Jessie Mae, the maid, and absolutely refused to give Chester the money, just as she had refused him the money to purchase Macon's old Lanier Hotel so that Fritz could manage it. Olivia Kyle later testified that Chester threatened to hit Mary with a telephone when she wouldn't give him money to buy the Lanier Hotel. At that point, in Olivia Kyle's presence, Mary insisted that she was going to write a letter to Fritz's family in New Jersey in order to "ruin him" socially. Chester screamed in response, "Would you expose him, Mary? Would you ruin our friendship?" Mary replied that she "wouldn't want a friendship like that." Fritz then packed for the two and they departed, discovering later that they had Mary's jewelry with them because she had left it in the coat pocket of Chester's suit.

Once Mary was back in Macon, she confronted Chester. He had told Olivia Kyle that Mary had "broken his back" by refusing to give him the $41,000 he needed to buy the Florida hotel. Chester also accused Mary of having cut him out of her will, and she responded that she had done so because Chester had made Fritz a beneficiary of his own will. These new wills had been drawn up on January 5. With conditions at a breaking point, Mary and their son, John, tried to reason with Chester. They explained that his relationship with Fritz was ruining their family. For his part, Fritz did not share the same level of emotional commitment but saw Chester as "an opportunity" to acquire his own hotel.

Chester was convinced by his family to seek medical help to cure the "sickness" of his attraction to men in general and to Fritz in particular. Chester agreed to investigate the possibility of undergoing a lobotomy in Switzerland to "cut out" the illness from his brain. As Fritz remembers, "He said that he and John had discussed the plan and that both of them were in accord about it but only if a doctor would recommend it." He and John decided that the eminent Dr. Corbett Thigpen* at the Medical College of Georgia in Augusta would be the perfect authority. As Fritz recalls, "That same doctor had just gained worldwide acclaim for having written the book which had just been released as a movie, called *The Three Faces of Eve*, starring Mrs. Paul Newman." The Georgia-born actress, Joanne Woodward, won an Academy Award for her 1957 performance as the patient suffering from multiple personality disorder.

Chester would only go to the scheduled appointment if Fritz would accompany him. Mary was decidedly unhappy

---

*   Dr. Corbett Thigpen (1919–99) was born in Macon and helped his family financially during the Depression by performing amateur magic acts for local civic clubs. After graduating from Mercer University and the Medical College of Georgia, he became one of only two professors at MCG teaching psychiatry. He wrote *The Three Faces of Eve* after having successfully treated the patient.

that she was not to be included. "Mr. Burge had made me promise that he would see the doctor only if I would go along. Mrs. Burge had agreed that the meeting was a good idea and perhaps things would be improved if the doctor would tell Mr. Burge what to do." As he recalls, "The drive to Augusta was uneventful and quiet . . . We showed up at his office, and the two of them met together while I waited outside. Then, finally I was invited in to speak with the two of them and the doctor simply spent the remainder of an hour telling me about homosexuality, and I must confess I had never been so uncomfortable. Finally he said that rather than have a drastic surgery that I should, for the good of all, simply go away from all of the Burges and then all of their problems would be solved." As Fritz listened to this eminent authority, "I must say that I was disappointed because the doctor told me that I was the reason that he, Mr. Burge, was gay and that I should leave the South and never come back. Of course that shot the plans for our trip to Europe all to hell." After such an intense relationship with Chester, "suddenly it was over. So was my immediate departure. Personally I was depressed because in my own mind, I was hanging in the breeze. I don't know what happened to them, but I did leave and Chester killed Mary."

The solution appeared logical to the Burges, says Fritz. "Chester and I had agreed to comply with whatever the advice was to be, so the die was cast. Frankly, I don't recall that John had any part in the decision, but Mary, Mrs. Burge, seemed resigned to the decision and expected no less from me, and so I did not disappoint her. John's opinion was not a factor and I just left—for good and for the good of all. My departure from the Burge house was a little solemn but at the same time genuinely warm and heartfelt. [Louis] hugged me; the laundress also hugged me, though I did wonder whether she had planned to squish me to death as I knew she could, and Mary kissed me farewell. Chester's farewell expression is lost as I have no memory at all of him at that point. So, back to New Jersey and marriage and farming and babies and house building and a completely new life with the Bedford family, my in-laws." But Fritz would see Chester once more.

Although Chester liked attention, he wasn't looking for the kind that came to him only two weeks before Mary's murder. On the night of April 26, the Ku Klux Klan came to light a cross on the lawn of the Burge home. Several local residents still recall the excitement of the evening. Among Chester's many real estate holdings in Macon was a house on Colquitt Street just off Antioch Road. At the time it was a white neighborhood, and Chester rented the house to a black family. The KKK wanted the Burges to force the black family out of the house and to promise to rent only to white tenants. Despite his secret relationship with his chauffeur, Chester was anything but an integrationist; the only color that mattered to him was green.

Estimates of the number of hooded KKK members ranged from forty to one hundred, with at least twice that number of attendees who gathered to watch the spectacle. Police were quickly called to maintain order. In a bow to modernity, the Klan intended to plug their electric cross into an outside receptacle rather than employ their normal practice of actually burning a wooden cross. But there was no outside electric source in the front of the Burge home. On the evening of the protest, Louis, the chauffeur, turned the Burge Cadillac quickly into the driveway, barely missing two men, who demanded that police arrest him. He was given a citation for reckless driving, but the charge was dropped when it reached Recorders Court on April 28. At the time Chester testified on Louis's behalf that, even on his nights off, Louis was often called to the residence at night to help care for Chester's aged mother, who lived with the Burges.

Seeking to restore order the night of the Klan rally, Mary came out of the house and sat on a stone wall conversing with R. Lee Davidson II, the Grand Dragon of the Georgia Ku Klux Klan.* While Mary was making progress, Chester came outside brandishing a loaded .38 caliber pistol. "Get off my property," he screamed, "and take your hooded hoodlums with you!" Police intervened and convinced Chester to go back into his house with his gun. Mary continued talking with the group's leader and assured him that if a white family could be found to rent the house in question, the Burges would evict the black family. At her murder only two weeks later, the Klan was immediately identified as a suspect.

On Sunday, May 8, Chester was visited at home by Russell Matthews, a former Macon City councilmember, and Louis Briggs, a contractor, who were there to discuss a possible business deal. While upstairs, Matthews "handled" Mary's pistol then gave it to Chester. It had been a gift to her from her son a few months earlier and was intended for her protection. Later in the day Chester checked into the Macon Hospital for a double hernia operation to be performed by Dr. Milford Hatcher

---

* The 9 February 1961 issue of *Jet* magazine quoted Davidson as having announced that part of his plan to halt integration in Georgia was to "move all Georgia negroes to Atlanta." Although he was short on details, he did maintain that it was part of his group's "secret weapon" to maintain segregation. Davidson would become Imperial Wizard of the Ku Klux Klan of America.

two days later. It was the same hospital where his father died after being accidentally struck by a black chauffeur. At the time, hospital stays for recuperation from surgery were considerably longer than they are today. Once Chester had sufficiently healed from his operation, he was scheduled to have an additional procedure to remove some moles from his lower legs, a toe, and his back.

Mrs. Sarah Durden, Chester's mother, lived with the couple, but she was away for several days visiting friends in nearby Perry, Georgia. She later testified that Chester called her to ask that she extend her trip a few days longer as they were having weekend guests, but he did not tell her he was scheduled for surgery during that time. Since February, Olivia and Edwin G. Kyle, cousins of Chester's mother at whose home in Tampa the confrontation with Mary had occurred, had been living in the apartment above the garage (later generously referred to as "guest quarters") with their three children. Louis, the chauffeur, no longer lived in his basement room since recently acquiring both a wife and his own apartment at 1361 Woodliff Street.

On Monday, amid laboratory tests and preparations for surgery, Chester signed a power of attorney for Mary to handle all the business affairs of their real estate and loan enterprises. Chester's surgery on Tuesday went well and he recovered as scheduled in his hospital room on the sixth floor. On Wednesday afternoon, May 11, the Burges' maid, Jessie Mae Holland, found Mary's beloved parrot bleeding in his cage. The bird lived on a porch in the back of the house, remembered the Lanneau sisters. He was loud and noisy and acted as a sort of watchdog for his mistress by "screeching" when others approached. He was so vicious that Chester and Mary's grandson, John Lee Burge, still has a fingertip mangled from when he tried to feed the parrot a bit of banana as a child. It was bandaged by the same Dr. Birdsong who was summoned when John's grandmother was murdered. On the afternoon of the day she died, Mary took the bird to the office of the family veterinarian, Dr. Herman Westmoreland, who tried unsuccessfully to treat it with a blood coagulant. But the bird died later anyway. Dr. Westmoreland later remembered, "The parrot despised yellow feathers and always plucked them out. Mary called me that afternoon and said, 'This bird looks dead, can I bring him over?' She brought it in one of those beer flats. He was in bad shape. He had hemorrhaged. I gave him something and sent them home, and that was the night she was murdered. A couple of days later some of her family called and asked me whether it could have been poisoned. They dug him up and several days later the report came back negative."* At the time, it was strongly suspected that the parrot had been poisoned. Even today, when the Burge murder is mentioned, those who recall it almost always mention the strange death of the parrot.

Something else unusual happened in the days leading up to Chester's surgery and Mary's murder. According to Rex Elder, owner of the neighborhood grocery where the Burges regularly traded, Mary "always came in herself and paid off her account on the last day of the month. Just before she was killed, she came in on what was not her usual day and said, 'I want to get everything in order.' She paid her account in cash

* Although Dr. Westmoreland was quietly homosexual, those who knew him doubt he would have perjured himself even if asked by Chester Burge. Dr. Angela Shurling, who trained under him and purchased his practice, confirms that it is quite possible for a bird to bleed to death if it pulls out a feather leading directly to a blood supply.

as she always did." Even then Elder thought it was unusual, so uncharacteristic of her routine practice. As soon as he learned of her murder, he realized that she knew something was going to happen to her.

That Wednesday evening, wearing her jewels, Mary visited Chester in his hospital room. She left him at 9:15, shortly after an announcement was made that visiting hours ended at 9:00. She drove directly to her home and, after parking her Cadillac, walked to the guest garage apartment to retrieve her grandson, John Lee, who was being cared for by the Kyles while she was away at the hospital. It was not known whether she may have first walked into her residence and perhaps left the door unlocked before entering the guest cottage. John Lee was seven and had been living with his grandparents since he was very young. Mary doted on him. They stayed with the Kyles for a few minutes to celebrate the couple's wedding anniversary.

Between 10:00 and 10:30, she and John Lee walked into the Burge residence and climbed the stairs. She readied him for bed, then put him to sleep in the room just down the hall from hers. Mary entered her own bedroom, undressed, and put on her nightgown and pink hairnet. The window was open to take advantage of any breeze from the river, although the shade on the window facing the guest cottage was closed. She folded her clothes neatly and placed them on a chair. On the nightstand next to her bed was her loaded .38 revolver. The diamond necklace she had worn that night was placed on the dresser. She had only minutes left to live.

Louis, the chauffeur, later testified that he left the Burge home late that night, locking the basement door behind him (he claimed not to have a key to the house). Shortly before

10:00 p.m. he went home to bed with his new wife. At ten minutes till midnight, he got up and went to the home of the maid, Jessie Mae Holland, at 134 Spring Street, where he remained until the next morning when he went to work at the Burge home later than she did. His late-night move would support an earlier inference from Louis's parole officer that Jessie Mae and Louis were sexually involved with one another. Or the possibility that Jessie Mae might provide an alibi for his actions that night.

Back at the hospital, at 9:00 Chester was given Demerol for pain, and at 9:30, just after Mary's departure, he took two sleeping pills from his nightstand drawer. Soon after Mary left, Chester had two visitors. The men were remembered as being "conspicuous" because they came after visiting hours had ended. Witnesses said "one was white and one was negro," and they did not stay long. The hospital spokesman later described them as "questionable-looking characters." At a little after 10:00 p.m., his physician, Dr. Milford Hatcher, looked into Chester's room from the hall. Because the room was dark he assumed that the figure he saw in bed was the sleeping Chester, so he did not enter the room to disturb him.

At a little past 7:00 a.m. the next morning, Thursday, May 12, Jessie Mae Holland let herself into the Burge residence through the kitchen door. She later said she used her key but didn't remember if she turned it, so Jessie Mae couldn't be certain whether the door was locked. Little John Lee was running a bit late, so she immediately got him dressed, fed him his breakfast, and got him out the door to walk to Alexander III school several blocks away. Mary was usually up in the morning, so Jessie Mae began to worry when she had not come down. At 8:55 a.m. she walked up the stairs and knocked lightly at Mary's door. When she received no reply, she opened the door. Mary Burge was lying in her antique four-poster bed with her head on the pillow. She was covered neatly with her bedclothes, but Jessie Mae could tell immediately that something was wrong. There were bruises on her right eye, her neck, and her hands. Fearing the worst, Jessie Mae went running to the guest cottage to summon the Kyles.

When the Kyles arrived, they knew immediately that Mary was dead. Edwin Kyle called the family physician, Dr. William Birdsong, who was making his morning rounds at the hospital. He asked Kyle to make sure that Mary was dead then come back to the phone. When the death was confirmed, Dr. Birdsong called the police and then immediately left for the residence. The coroner was called. The sheriff was called, and he called the Bibb County medical examiner. The Kyles called the Burges' son, John, who was then teaching economics at Auburn University. Meanwhile, the newly widowed Chester lay uninformed in his hospital bed, having had an uneventful morning.

Shortly before noon, a nurse bathed him. She later testified that she noticed no marks, cuts, or abrasions other than his surgical incision. While she was still in the room, Chester reached over and turned on his bedside radio. In an interview he gave the next day to Hal Gulliver* of the *Atlanta Constitution*, Chester described how he heard of his wife's murder.

---

* Gulliver would have a long and distinguished career in journalism. In 1971 he cowrote, with Reg Murphy, a critically acclaimed book explaining Richard Nixon's successful "Southern strategy," calculated to appeal to white segregationist sentiment in order to move the South from the Democratic to the Republican column.

"The nurse had finished bathing me and I was listening to the radio. The nurse wasn't even listening to the news. I think I screamed . . . my God, I kept hoping she'd only been beaten up." When Gulliver visited Chester in his hospital room the next day, he watched him listening to the radio. "As a news broadcast began, he turned the radio up slightly, closed his eyes, and listened to the latest account of the murder, his chest moving quickly with his rapid breathing." Chester exclaimed to the reporter, "To think we're living in the twentieth century. They must have been fiends. And my home is three minutes' drive from the courthouse!"

When Chester learned of his wife's murder, he said, "I wanted to go home as soon as I heard and I promised to come right back to the hospital. My son got there about fifteen minutes after I did." The fact that Auburn was a two-and-a-half-hour drive from Macon gives a good impression of how long John learned of his mother's death before Chester did. The new widower was taken to his home by ambulance and, through a side door, was carried inside on a stretcher at 12:29 p.m. without giving the press an opportunity to see or photograph him. While at home for about forty-five minutes, he was asked to determine what might be missing. "There were two diamond clips from her jewel box gone and approximately $5,000." Describing how his wife appeared, Chester said, "It was hideous to look at. Brutal. I never saw anything so horrible. The fiends almost tore her finger off trying to get a ring. My God, I can't believe it!"

Of his wife, Chester declared to Gulliver, "She was a beautiful woman, a wonderful hostess. She liked to help people. She was a very charitable woman. She liked to help people who were too proud to ask for help. There is a portrait of her in the drawing room. Go look at the portrait. She was beautiful." Chester had ordered that Mary's body not be moved until he could see her. Shortly after he left the house, she was taken to Hart's Mortuary at 1:06 p.m. The work of the detectives had barely started, although Mary's murder had already been announced as a probable robbery.

One of the first police officers on the scene was Frank Lanneau. In fact, he was the officer who accompanied Chester into Mary's bedroom. Lanneau and his family were very familiar with the Burge home. Not only did Frank's elder daughter, Marie, babysit for little John Lee, but the younger daughter, Kay, was one of his playmates. Chester Burge actually held the mortgage on the Lanneaus' home. Harry Harris, who worked for the Bibb County Sheriff's office for more than forty years, was assigned to the case to help the Macon police at the request of the district attorney, Bill West. Although there was known corruption in the Macon Police Department, Harris said of Frank Lanneau, "He was honest, but he was a nine-to-five man. He made his money as a cabinetmaker."

Frank Lanneau's widow, Erma, explained that, early in their marriage, she and Frank had chosen a site to build their house not far from both Lanier High School, where their son would attend, and Miller High School, where their two daughters would attend. At the time, not only were Macon's schools segregated by race, but white boys and girls attended separate high schools as well. The Lanneaus had chosen the building site and planned to buy it for back taxes when it came up for auction. When that day came, however, they learned that Chester Burge had already bought it.

Erma Lanneau was a persistent woman and had her heart set on that site, so she called Chester even though she didn't know him. He had paid $250 for the lot and agreed to sell it to the Lanneaus for $500. They needed what was, to them on a policeman's salary, a large amount of money in order to build the house. Chester obligingly lent them the money and they paid him back at $35 per month over the life of the mortgage. So the first police officer on the scene and one of the principal police officers who investigated Chester's complicity in his wife's murder paid his monthly mortgage payment to Chester.

The Lanneaus became friendly with the Burges, though certainly not intimate. As Erma said, "We used to go swim in their pool. I had three children and they had one of the few pools in Macon." For their part, the girls recall that "Mrs. Burge was a beautiful, kind woman," and Erma agreed that Chester "was always kind and sweet to me and to the children." In fact, on one occasion, said the diminutive Erma, Chester "brought me three nice dresses from a business trip he took north, but they were all size 20! I gave them to a friend who was big."

Erma thought it somewhat odd that "the Burges didn't have many friends." But she was adamant about Chester's feelings for little John Lee. "He loved that boy. He had a bad medical problem when he was little—his stomach—but he got better." Perhaps tellingly, Erma recalled, "I liked Mr. Burge more than Frank did, but maybe, because of his work, Frank knew things about him that I didn't." Marie remembers, "There was a pearl necklace theft that was probably insurance fraud. The police were called to investigate the theft. They found the pearls outside the bedroom window on the ground." Marie also recalls, "Mr. Burge's mother, who was at the house a lot, told my mother Chester 'kicked Mary in the shins till she bled' to get money and what he wanted." Marie insists of Mary's murder,

"She would not have gone down without a fight. Mary was a determined woman. John Lee was down the hall from her sleeping the night she was murdered. She would have wanted to protect John Lee. Her left ring finger was nearly torn off the night of her death. The murderer wanted her large diamond to make it look like a robbery."

Marie's assumption that Mary did not go down without a fight is quite correct.

CHAPTER SEVEN

In the pre–Civil Rights era of central Georgia, homosexuality was a completely forbidden topic. Jordan Massee remembered of his own adolescence in Macon, "Boys learned of sexual practices from other boys, unusual practices as well as usual. The information was passed up from the lower socioeconomic levels, unlike today when such sophisticated knowledge trickles down. As for activity, poor boys were more likely preyed upon; and, of course, farm boys got the earliest start." One of his memories from the all-male high school (where he called his own experience "five years in hell") is particularly chilling: "The principal of Lanier High School for Boys was expelled. The majority of the students were aware of his proclivities long before he was caught *in flagrante*. He frequently beat the boys unmercifully, with obvious pleasure. The combination of homosexuality and sadism sent shock waves through the community." Massee was firmly of the belief that, "Homosexual activity is dependent on acceptance and availability. Repression leads to secrecy and sublimation; neither gets counted. I wonder why antebellum houses had no closets."

Dr. Herman Westmoreland, the veterinarian who treated the Burges' parrot, remembers the early days of "gay" life in Macon: "Everybody was very much in the closet; nothing was open then. We had a few old lecherous things like Chester Burge, who was notorious for his young men."[*]

---

[*] I am indebted to Phil Comer for allowing me access to a recorded audiotape interview with the late Dr. Herman Westmoreland.

As sheriff's investigator Harry Harris said of Chester Burge's sex life at the time, "Macon knew it but Macon didn't talk about it." Lisa Davis has a unique perspective on the subject, as well as on the events surrounding Mary's murder. After earning her PhD, she is now a respected author and lecturer in New York City. But from the fall of 1959 until the spring of 1960, she was a student at Mercer University "and came out to meet the gay community of Macon" as she now recalls. It is a great understatement to say that the community was well hidden. There was only one place for gays to congregate, and that was the old Ann's Tic Toc Room in downtown Macon. Harry Harris remembered that "the chauffeur took Chester to Ann's Tic Toc Room and he would go in through the back door." The lounge was also one of the few places where blacks and whites could easily mingle, and it was there that Macon's own Little Richard began to perform (born Richard Penniman, he started as a "drag baby," calling himself "Princess Lavonne," dressed in red and wearing high heels). In fact, the Georgia Music Hall of Fame, the state's official music museum located in Macon, displays the piano that Little Richard played at the Tic Toc Room.*

Even as a student on the fringes of Macon's gay community, Davis quickly heard when investigating police discovered that Chester was "gay and involved with many shady characters. From that point on, the investigation mushroomed, and many of Macon's gay citizens were dragged down to the police station, fingerprinted, etc. As a student at Mercer, I survived the purge, but a friend of mine did not. She was apprehended

---

* The Tic Toc Room was restored several years ago and now offers an elegant restaurant as well as a trendy night club greatly favored by Macon's college students for an "upscale" evening.

at the notorious Ann's Tic Toc Lounge. . . forced to show a Mercer I.D., and summarily thrown out of school." She was only weeks away from graduating.

Davis recalls that, just after the murder, "the police would round up anybody they could find." She also says that, at the time, there were "a lot of working-class lesbians in Macon" who toiled at blue-collar jobs and were not students. As she says now, "They were really nice gals but, you know, not the sort Mercer coeds were supposed to be dating. They were very good to me." Although Davis stayed away from the Tic Toc, she did attend all girls' softball games "with the 'working class' set." Among those she knew were two women who were lovers, Jo and Shirley, both of whom were nurses. Shirley was a friend of an attractive young man named Quinton "Sandy" Dent, who was also gay. Davis recalls him vividly: "Sandy was, indeed, quite beautiful. Blonde, blue (I suppose)-eyed, the all-American boy but always determined to shock the hell out of everybody. The first time I met him in that apartment with the hall painted black, he was dancing to some rock and roll music clad only in short shorts. Shirley, on the other hand, was not a beautiful girl—short and chubby, rather dumpy. I can't imagine her at a Chester party with all the slender sophisticates. Sandy, of course, would have been right at home there, or in Buckingham Palace."

Shirley and Sandy were on Chester's Christmas card list and attended his large parties, although, as Davis recalls, "Chester, of course, only wanted Sandy." Eventually, in what Davis assumes was "just one of those arrangements," Shirley and Sandy married. Lisa recalls that Sandy's "parents came for dinner soon after his marriage to Shirley and their move to the apartment on the hill with the hallway painted black. Shirley had prepared a lovely dinner and was making nice with the in-laws, who must have wondered. Sandy was nowhere to be found until everyone sat down at the table, which had a metal frame and a clear glass top. Sandy appeared wearing only a jockstrap (I suppose it was a warm day) and plopped down at the table. His parents were somewhat chagrined, not to mention Shirley."

As luck—or perhaps good planning—would have it, Shirley was working on the hospital floor where Chester was recuperating on the night of Mary's murder, and perhaps Jo was as well. The on-duty nurses from that night would become part of the case at trial, and their testimony was relied on by both sides. Shirley may well have played a role in Chester's activities that evening. Both Sandy and Shirley are now deceased.

As Lisa Davis indicates, the pressure was on for Macon police to find a suspect in Mary's murder. Fingers pointed immediately at the Ku Klux Klan because of their rally at the Burge home only weeks before. But Lee Davidson, the Grand Dragon of the Georgia Klan who had conversed with Mary the night of the rally, said publicly, "I'm just dumbfounded. I don't know what to think." On the issue of any Klan involvement in the murder, Davidson said, you can "erase that from your mind."

Perhaps because they were black, or because they had criminal backgrounds, Louis the chauffeur, Jessie Mae the maid, and Gene the former chauffeur were all arrested "on open charges" the day after Mary's body was discovered. They were not given an attorney. Jessie Mae was released after a few hours, but Louis and Gene continued to be held. A couple of days later, three more black residents who had been involved in renting the Burge properties protested by the Klan were also arrested "on open charges." It was thought sufficient that they lived in the neighborhood where the disputed rental house was located. One reported that a brick had been thrown through his window on the night of the Ku Klux Klan rally. When Chester was told the black suspects were being held, he replied that Mary had "helped Negroes . . . It would be hard to believe [the murderer] was a Negro. She bought milk for indigent Negroes. I didn't know anyone who was her enemy."

Dr. Leonard H. Campbell, the medical examiner (and a close friend of Chester's son, John), and Coroner Lester Chapman told waiting reporters outside the Burge residence on the day after the murder that Mary's death from strangulation happened about midnight and that there were "marks" on and around her face. Dr. Campbell also announced that Mary's finger on which she wore her large diamond was "almost severed from the hand, apparently in an effort to remove the ring." Detective Frank Lanneau announced that an unsuccessful attempt had been made to enter a "locked room" (actually, a walk-in closet) "where Burge kept a large amount of cash and other valuables." He stressed that the Burges operated their business from their home and that many people passed through the house.

One police source said that some of the neighborhood boys reported having heard "a prowler in the bushes" near the rear of the house shortly before midnight. That announcement included a reminder that the Burges had less than two years earlier reported the theft of two diamond necklaces, totaling seventy-seven carats and valued at more than $25,000, that were sent to Mary on approval from an Atlanta jeweler. The thief had supposedly entered the house by breaking a pane of glass on the front door, then reaching inside and opening it. A couple of days after the theft the Burges' yard man found the necklaces tossed into shrubbery outside the house.

Friday the thirteenth was not a lucky day for Chester. Mary's death, as well as his family business, was spread all over the front page of the newspaper. It was also the day police first hinted at possible motives other than theft. Chief of Detectives W. H. Bargeron announced, "Robbery is not the only thing we are considering . . . There may be some possible loss from the house, but we are not sure about this." Even for those officers who were not long-acquainted with Chester's reputation, it would have taken only hours to learn about it from any number of sources. Surely someone at headquarters would have remembered that he had been detained for soliciting sex in the men's room of the Lanier Hotel. Bargeron also confirmed that Mary's grandson, John Lee, heard nothing during the night and only learned of her death when he returned from school that afternoon. There was no one waiting with open arms and sympathy to explain that his beloved grandmother was dead.

Police suspicion was enhanced when Chester's cousin, Olivia Kyle, told them about her conversation with Chester shortly after he learned of Mary's death but before he was taken to the house. He called her to his hospital bed to ask about the death scene. She related their conversation: "He told me it was robbery, and I told him, 'No, they didn't take anything.' He said, 'But what about the ring?' I said, 'But they found the stone.'" Burge then yelled at her, "Get out! Get out!" She did leave but returned a few minutes later when he told her not to allow Mary's body to be moved until he arrived at home. Although Olivia Kyle was Chester's mother's cousin, it was obvious early on that she took Mary's side, as did Chester's own mother, who eventually was to testify against him. The family dynamics were not what was usually expected in a brutal murder investigation.

On Friday, Dr. Leonard Campbell, the medical examiner, announced that Mary Burge died "some time about midnight" and that the cause of death was "strangulation with intent to kill." He also announced that she was not sexually assaulted. Her assailant, Campbell concluded, caught her with both hands by the throat from behind. A bone in her throat was fractured, and deep pressure damage was found in the skin tissues of her neck. She had a cut on her left hand, bruises and a cut on her face, bruises on her back, and fingernail marks on her throat. Those latter marks, however, were made by Mary herself as she tried to loosen the killer's hands around her throat. Chief Detective Bargeron was of the opinion that Mary had already prepared for bed and put on her nightgown and may have been walking back into her bedroom from the bathroom (which adjoined Chester's bedroom as well) when the attack occurred.

Police also announced that Mary's bedroom floor, which was carpeted, showed signs of a struggle and had a bloodstain on it. The detectives said she "may already have been dead at the time she was put on the bed." Her pillow had a bloodstain that had been smeared, as though she had been moved there after her death and the covers partially pulled up over her body. This announcement also included the first mention of a closet door that would become vital to the case. This was the locked closet, which held cash and valuables, and the pin to one of the hinges on the door had supposedly been partially knocked out "possibly using a screwdriver and blows of one hand." The attempt to open the door was unsuccessful, and there were paint chips from it that had fallen to the floor. Newspaper accounts included the observation that the reporter "found valuable silver and antiques in perfect order throughout the big two-story building."

Mary's funeral service was announced for Saturday, May 14, at 4:30 p.m. at Christ Episcopal Church, one of the most elite churches in the city. Her body was brought home at noon the day before the funeral and remained there overnight. The list of honorary pallbearers was impressive both for its number and its influence. Among the twenty-four men were Fritz's uncle, Newbold Hutchinson, who had introduced him to Chester; the "fashionable" attorney William Turpin; next-door neighbor P. L. Hay Jr.; Jo-Lynn's father and brother; family physician Dr. W. R. Birdsong; Dr. Milford Hatcher, who performed Chester's surgery; Mayor Ed Wilson; Arnold Jacobs, who was to be one of Chester's attorneys; and E. J. Kyle, the husband of Chester's cousin Olivia, who had first been summoned to find Mary's body. Chester was rolled into the church in his wheelchair directly behind Mary's coffin. The sanctuary was packed for the service, and Laura Nelle O'Callaghan recalled that Chester "went to the funeral at Christ Church and he was the biggest mourner there. And a few days after that they arrested him for it."

Even with Fritz's uncle as a pallbearer, no one thought to inform Fritz of Mary's death. He doesn't recall exactly who eventually told him of the murder, but "with all of the unrest that Mr. Burge had caused, there was an embargo on Burge-Macon talk in the households of New Jersey. It seems to me, though, that someone completely unrelated to the events had seen the article in the Macon paper and casually mentioned

it. It was, and it wasn't, a surprise when I heard about it."
When asked to explain that contradiction, Fritz elaborates, "I
was stricken with remorse when I heard of her murder but
soon reverted to, 'What else could she expect in a marriage
like that?' It was the laying-down-with-dogs-and-fleas thing.
My greatest dismay was that the detectives even courted the
notion that Chester was innocent."

Mary's body was placed in the mausoleum of Riverside
Cemetery, where her first son was interred, rather than in the
hallowed ground of the adjoining Rose Hill Cemetery. Chester
was driven back to the hospital after the interment, and it was
reported that several police officers attended the ceremony
when "it appeared they were trying to spot someone among
the people." That day's newspaper carried the police theory
that "the attack was probably by just one person. They think
he may have used a key to get in, since no mark of forcible
entry was found anywhere in the house." Bargeron also theorized that Mary was surprised by the intruder before getting
into bed and did not have time to reach for her loaded pistol.

Mourners and family members returned home to find the
afternoon newspaper waiting with two front-page stories. One,
titled CONTROVERSY HITS BURGES: SERIES OF LAWSUITS, was a recitation of
the family's history of litigation and legal wrangling. The other,
however, was far more subtle. Buried deep within the story's
chronological listing of the details of the murder was this statement: "The detectives have already relegated robbery to a secondary position among possible motives, although they have
declined to specify the new motive on which they are concentrating." Another interesting revelation was that the killer
placed Mary on her bed after the murder because he may have
wished "to get out of the view of a window and to finish the

job. The murderer may have thought she was not dead when he put her on the bed and he wanted to make sure."

Sunday morning's newspaper blared the headline Was Burge Parrot Poisoned to Death? Loud Squawking Silenced. Portions of the pet's body were sent to the state crime lab in Atlanta for analysis. The coroner had also changed his mind about the murder weapon, having decided that Mary's murderer did not use his bare hands but "an instrument which was strong, pliable, soft, and would not leave any mark."

Monday brought a re-arrest of Jessie Mae Holland, the maid who had been questioned briefly and released on the day after the murder. Louis, the chauffeur, was driven to Atlanta, administered a lie detector test, and returned in the afternoon to Macon, where he continued to be held. On Tuesday, more suspicion was aroused when police disclosed that the Burges' setter dog, Boy, had been shut up in the basement the night of the murder. The dog was given to little John Lee by his father during a visit in February and left there as his companion. A detective heard the dog whining behind the closed door when searching the house on the day the murder was discovered. When informed that the dog had been locked in the basement, Mary's son, John, said he "could not necessarily attach any significance one way or another" to the matter, since the dog "often slept in the basement because the furnace is there and the place is warm." Local residents were convinced that the reports of both the dog and the parrot added up to premeditation by someone who was very familiar with the household. That same day's afternoon newspaper ended its respectful tone in reporting the Burge murder, referring to Chester in print as "an ex-bootlegger who has amassed considerable wealth." Clearly something was up.

Seven days after Mary's murder, police were still awaiting reports from the crime lab in Atlanta as well as results from Louis's lie detector test. John personally presented his mother's will at the Bibb County Courthouse with a hearing for probate set for June 6. The will was not, as Chester had said it was, a joint will of husband and wife. Chester was also incorrect in stating publicly that John would have to resign his teaching position at Auburn and become a Macon resident in order to serve as executor of his mother's estate. Attorneys determined that he could teach anywhere so long as he listed Bibb County as his legal address. Chester was also incorrect that his son would have to post a one-million-dollar bond if he did not move home to handle his mother's estate. Perhaps the father was trying to manipulate the son. It would not be the last time.

Mary's will was very specific in leaving two trusts to benefit her husband and her son, both to be administered by the C&S Bank. John was to receive the house, and at his death, the trust was to benefit his children. That point would eventually become an issue for Chester and Mary's grandchildren. Estate and inheritance taxes were to be paid from John's estate, although he was to live rent-free and the trust was to pay all taxes, repairs, and operating expenses for the house. Chester, still in Macon Hospital on the day John presented his mother's will at the courthouse, had some cancerous skin growths removed as planned.

Despite pronouncements that police were working sixteen-hour days to break the case, a full week after the murder nothing seemed more definite than it had on the day after it occurred. Chester went to the office of Chief of Detectives W. H. Bargeron to discuss "a personal matter." Although Bargeron also had a conversation with John Burge, there was no disclosure of what either conversation entailed. By that time the strain between Chester and the police was becoming public.

On Thursday afternoon, a full week after the murder, Chester called reporters to his hospital room. With his son by his bedside, Chester waited ten or fifteen minutes past the appointed hour because he expected both Detective Bargeron and Sheriff James I. Wood to appear. When it became obvious they would not attend, Chester said the sheriff was "probably out politicking." He then proceeded to read the following signed statement:

"My son and I do hereby offer a $5,000 reward for the arrest and conviction of the person or persons responsible for the murder of Mrs. Mary E. Burge." It was signed by both Chester and John. When Detective Bargeron was later asked why he had skipped Chester's announcement, he replied that it was no concern of his and he was too busy to attend. That same afternoon, Chester told a reporter, "I had hoped to go on a trip to Europe very soon. But I'm not sure now whether I'll be able to go or not, since all this terrible business has come up." His plans had called for him to leave Macon on May 29 for a sailing date from New York City of June 6. But Chester wasn't going anywhere for a long time.

CHAPTER EIGHT

On Friday, May 20, the same day that Chester's reward announcement was reported in the newspapers, he was arrested. He was dismissed from Macon Hospital at 1:40 p.m. still wearing his pajamas, bathrobe, and slippers. Police had instructed John not to take his father home but to bring him directly to police headquarters for questioning. Because he could not climb stairs, Chester was carried up in a chair by police officers. They questioned him for four hours, sometimes in the presence of Louis, the chauffeur, and sometimes with Gene, the former chauffeur, who were both being held downstairs in a cell.

At 6:15 that evening, Chester Burge was booked "on open charges," docketed, fingerprinted, and taken directly to a cell still wearing his pajamas and robe, although clothes were later brought to him. When Chief Detective Bargeron was asked whether Chester would be held for only a few hours or perhaps longer, he replied, "I fully expect him to be here in the morning." Within minutes Arnold Jacobs, an attorney who had served as one of Mary's pallbearers, arrived to confer with Chester. He said he was there "as an old friend" and had not been retained to represent the accused. John was asked by reporters what he thought of his father's arrest, and he responded only by saying that he thought police were "using all their facilities" in investigating his mother's death.

Because the next day was Sunday, there could be no legal appeal to a court for habeas corpus to secure Chester's release. Bargeron used the opportunity to question him again for a further three hours. At the conclusion of that session, Bargeron announced to waiting reporters that Chester had refused to take a lie detector test. Despite Arnold Jacobs's presence at the jail the day before, no one had yet been retained to represent Chester. When queried, Bargeron said, "I haven't heard from his lawyers today, and I don't know of any procedure they've taken to get Burge released." The *Macon Telegraph* could not refrain from reporting, "Apparently detectives are either stumped at the present about the murder case or they are gathering more evidence in the case before charging anyone." Although it was pointed out that Chester had been held for forty-eight hours and would have to be charged soon or released, the two black chauffeurs had already been in jail for ten days. Also on Sunday, two detectives, Paul Kozee and J. W. Powell, left on an airplane for a trip of "several hundred miles," it was reported, to question someone in connection with the murder.

It hadn't taken police long to come across Fritz's name in their investigation. The detectives flew up to New Jersey to interview him, and Fritz vividly recalls of the meeting, "They were accusatory; they said I'd done it." Of course it was easy for him to prove that he had not been near Georgia at the time of Mary's murder. But police still suspected him of complicity. "They asked if I'd take a lie detector test and I said sure. All the homosexuality had to come out and that wasn't done at the time. Now it doesn't matter." Since police were armed with that evidence, Fritz had little alternative except to do what they asked. "I came down afterwards. I don't think they had a subpoena or my family wouldn't have let me go alone. They just wanted me to come down and confront him. They said 'We know he did it but we don't have any proof.'"

Fritz was first taken into a room at police headquarters where he saw John. "I recall that when John came into the room, I had expected to see his father, so I suspect that the detectives had wanted to watch my response to our meeting. I was deeply hurt when he didn't take my offered hand . . . I was really shocked then I remembered, 'Well, after all it was his mother who was killed.' . . . Then after a terrible pause I think that he left the room . . . I felt betrayed a little when he rejected my friendship at our only meeting after the tragedy. I wanted to comfort him as any friend would."

Next was the ultimate confrontation—facing Chester. "When Chester was brought into the room, I had been instructed by the detectives to ask him point blank, 'Why did you kill Mary?'" Chester looked directly back at Fritz "with affection in his eyes" and replied, "'Why did you do it?' And I said, 'You gotta be crazy!'" As Fritz looked at him, "all that I could remember is how much I detested him for doing such an unnatural thing. I just couldn't think that anyone I knew would do such a thing like that." After the confrontation, Fritz recalls of Chester, "He looked deflated—not the cocky bantam rooster that he was." Fritz never again saw Chester or his son. Although he was a frequent topic at the trial, he was not called to testify.

Fritz was quite correct in stating that the police officers told him of Chester, "We know he did it but we don't have any proof." At this point, they were desperate and determined that someone as depraved as Chester deserved to pay for his crimes, no matter what they were.

After Chester's arrest and a two-night stay in jail, he was returned to Macon Hospital. But this time he traded in his familiar room for one on the seventh floor—the psychiatric ward. A guard was placed at his door and he was considered to be in police custody. By this time, Arnold Jacobs was officially acting as Chester's attorney and announced that he "was admitted to the hospital for psychiatric observation at the request of his attending physician."

One report that he had been given a "truth serum" could not be confirmed by official sources. Although Chief Detective Bargeron said on Wednesday that, if Chester was getting any truth serum, Bargeron was unaware of it, the Wednesday afternoon paper blared as its headline: BURGE GETS DOSES OF HYPNOTIC DRUGS: INJECTIONS ARE BEING GIVEN BY PSYCHIATRIST. The combination of scopolamine and amytal was said to produce a "twilight sleep" under which a subject would be enticed to tell the truth. Bargeron, however, said, "I know nothing about it. I haven't even heard it mentioned." Chester's readmission to the hospital was said to have been approved by his son, John, as was the use of a hypnotic drug. The medicinal combination was reported to have been used "to learn the identity of amnesia victims, in childbirth, and for combat shock and fatigue in wartime." Bargeron said that, if Chester was under the influence of those drugs, "He didn't show it and we didn't know it." He did qualify that statement, however, by saying that, while it would be "unethical" for police to question Chester while under the influence of drugs, it would be perfectly normal for that to happen while being questioned by his psychiatrist (who was almost certainly Dr. Z. S. Sikes, assisted by Dr. J. R. Shannon Mays). That same story revealed that an unnamed Fritz had been questioned in New Jersey, and that the two men who had visited Chester after Mary's departure on the night she was murdered—"a white man and a negro"—had been located and questioned.

As the murder probe moved into its third week, residents turned their attention to other matters. Newspaper reporting on the case was moved to inside stories or, at most, small sidebars on the front page. Fritz was finally named as someone police had spoken with about the case, but little else was new, and attention waned.

The Democratic Party was moving closer to nominating a young and vibrant senator from Massachusetts, John F. Kennedy, as president. During the early primaries Kennedy was attacked for his Catholic faith, but that was not an issue in Georgia, where the Catholic governor of New York, Al Smith, received 56 percent of the vote when he was the Democratic nominee for president in 1928. Only one week before Mary's murder, Kennedy decisively defeated Hubert Humphrey in the first televised debate of the 1960 presidential election. Although Georgia had no primary, interest in a handsome young man with a beautiful wife had far more appeal than following a local murder case that seemed to be going nowhere.

Everything changed on the morning of June 1, when the *Macon Telegraph* moved the story back to page one with two accompanying photos of Chester and the headline Burge Is Charged With Murder of Wife. In announcing the charge the day before, Chief Detective Bargeron claimed, "We do know and can prove that he was in his home on the night of the murder. He could have been there 45 minutes . . . or an hour . . . or up to two hours." This news was incendiary. Police were claiming that Chester, having had a double hernia operation less than forty-eight hours earlier, and under the effects of two doses of sedatives, somehow left the hospital undetected, went home, murdered his wife, and returned to his bed. Bargeron even specified that police could place him in Mary's bedroom on the night of the murder, and stated that Chester had again refused to take a lie detector test. Bargeron announced gravely, "In my opinion Mrs. Burge's murder was premeditated and was planned a long time in advance."

Bargeron knew how to influence public opinion by what information he released and, early on, began to paint Chester in the darkest terms possible without directly accusing him of additional crimes. He insisted publicly, "There was nothing to that report of $5,000 cash being taken from the room. That was never mentioned by Burge after the first day." His insinuations to reporters eager to garner information led to such unattributed statements as this: "Acquaintances of the couple said there was considerable disagreement between Mr. and Mrs. Burge on both business and personal affairs. But detectives declined to discuss it."

The *Telegraph* reporter, Alice Price Crawford*, either had her own police sources or took great initiative in seeking out the story. She noted in her reporting that Chester's "hospital room on the sixth floor was a corner room at the end of corridor, and a staircase was located just around the corner from it. Without going past the main nursing station, that staircase would be easily accessible from the room. And it led to a fire door on the ground floor near Hemlock Street. Self-service elevators also provide transportation between floors of the big hospital. On the late night shift, **fewer than half dozen nurses and aides have the care of some 50 patients on the sixth floor.**" [Boldface is hers.] Crawford was already making the prosecution's case for them.

---

* A 1940 graduate of Wesleyan College, Crawford was clearly effective as a crime reporter in what was still considered a "man's job."

Evidently one nurse who was working on Chester's floor the night of Mary's murder quit her employment at the hospital shortly after the crime occurred. The hospital's administrative director insisted, however, that her departure "had absolutely nothing to do with this case. Nothing whatever. The nurse had already resigned, for personal reasons, long before Burge even entered the hospital. She was just working out her notice."

On the day he was charged with his wife's murder, Chester was driven from the hospital to police headquarters, calling waiting news photographers "vultures." Still in his same pajamas and robe, he was questioned for five hours. Minutes after the murder charge was announced, Chester's son, John, and his attorney arrived at headquarters but would not speak with reporters. Although Chester was still held in a police cell, he was scheduled to be moved to the Bibb County jail.

By the afternoon newspaper's edition, Bargeron had stepped up his onslaught upon Chester's reputation. The headline screamed BURGE 'HATED HIS WIFE,' CHIEF OF DETECTIVES SAYS. The lead sentence also included Bargeron's statement that Mary was murdered by Chester because "she had interfered with his private life." When pressed, the detective would not explain his statement. He did, however, admit that Fritz's presence in questioning Burge "had helped considerably in winding up the murder probe." The *Macon News* reporter, Charles Salter, did not cite his source in stating, "the investigation has disclosed that Burge had once planned to take Phillips [Fritz] to Europe but the plans had been cancelled. Another source said that Burge had decided to take a Macon acquaintance who has not been identified to Europe instead."

That same day came the first public mention that Chester was negotiating to retain the two hottest trial attorneys in Macon to represent him. Two years earlier, Charles Adams and Hank O'Neal successfully prosecuted Anjette Lyles. She was convicted of the murder of her nine-year-old daughter and was implicated in the murder of her two husbands and her mother-in-law. Anjette ran a restaurant in downtown Macon that was popular with the courthouse crowd, and her murder weapon of choice, perhaps unsurprisingly, was arsenic-poisoned food. Although sentenced to die in the electric chair, she was later adjudged "psychotic and insane" and sent to the state's asylum in Milledgeville (the same one where Chester was held early in his life) where she worked in the cafeteria before dying of heart failure in 1977.

Adams and O'Neal were successful in prosecuting her largely because they were able to introduce the other deaths to indicate a pattern even though Anjette was not on trial for those murders. They also presented evidence that Anjette would take food and drink to the victims while they were in the hospital, disappear into the restroom for a few minutes, taking both the drink and her purse with her, and then give the drink to her victim. A witness testified that, when Anjette's little daughter was in a hospital bed crying out from hallucination-induced terror, her mother laughed at her rather than attempt to console her. Two weeks before the girl's death, during a period when her doctors were predicting her recovery, Anjette ordered a coffin for her. At the same time, Anjette packed up the girl's personal belongings in her hospital room, discarded the flowers, and said, "Well, she won't be using these anymore." Obviously such distressing testimony had its intended effect on the jury. Adams and O'Neal normally were defense attorneys, but Solicitor General Bill West recused himself because of a distant relationship to the defendant, and the two were appointed to prosecute Anjette.*

Bill Adams, judge of the State Court of Bibb County in Macon, remembers that his father, Charles Adams, and Hank O'Neal met with Chester on both June 1 and June 2 to discuss their terms for representing him. They knew of Chester's unsavory character and, in effect, were holding all the cards in the negotiations. When Adams told Chester that they would represent him for $50,000, according to Bill Adams, Chester responded, "there was no way he was going to pay them that much money to defend him. Dad told Mr. O'Neal, 'Let's go' and they picked up their papers and started walking down the hall away from Burge. As they walked away, Mr. O'Neal was telling Dad that maybe they quoted too high a fee and they should consider charging something less. Dad said no and they kept walking away. About that time Burge hollered at them to come back and he agreed to pay them a $50,000 fee. The rest, as they say, is history." The two joined Arnold Jacobs, who was already working for Chester's defense. Although the amount Chester paid was unprecedented in Macon in 1960, it would be money well spent. In announcing that the three attorneys would represent Chester, they issued a joint statement asserting, "Mr. Burge maintains his complete innocence of the murder of his wife, and upon the call for trial of this case his plea will be not guilty. We are encouraged by statements of the detectives that they will continue to investigate this case. It gives rise to the hope that the guilty party will eventually be found and brought to justice."

---

* An informative account of the case can be found in *Whisper to the Black Candle: Voodoo, Murder, and the Case of Anjette Lyles*, Jaclyn W. White, Mercer University Press, 1999.

Chester had been delivered to the Bibb County jail and the official coroner's inquest delayed "until all details of the investigation are wrapped up." When his request for a television in his cell was denied, he objected that Anjette Lyles had been allowed a television. His jailer told him that she was given that privilege only after she was sentenced to die.

An examination of Bibb County tax records showed that the Burges owned more than one-half million dollars in real estate in the county, and that figure did not include any jewelry or personal property. That disclosure would attract the attention of the Internal Revenue Service, who had cause to wonder how such an accumulation was possible given the Burges' reported joint income of approximately five thousand dollars per month.

Chester's attorneys immediately set about to earn their fee. They filed a writ of habeas corpus claiming that he was being "illegally and unlawfully restrained of his liberty" and that he was "languishing in custody" since his arrest on May 20 with no commitment hearing to determine his fate. As a result, a hearing was finally scheduled for June 9; Chester and his attorneys would at last be able to hear the evidence against him. The coroner still had not scheduled an inquest, so nothing that the authorities had that might prove Chester's guilt or innocence was available to him or to his attorneys. Chief Detective Bargeron also announced that he had no plans to call a grand jury session to hear the evidence in order to present an indictment. He had no intention of tipping his hand.

On Sunday newspaper readers were given a basic education in the legal system as it related to Chester's case. The habeas corpus hearing scheduled for the following Thursday morning was being held, it was claimed, so that his attorneys could learn what evidence had been collected against him. If it was not sufficient, Chester's release would be ordered. If it was substantial, however, at least the defense team would know the particulars and begin preparations to refute it. There was to be a regularly scheduled meeting of a current grand jury the following morning, but Bargeron had made known no intention of presenting evidence to them. Should that grand jury, however, hear the evidence and indict Chester, then the Thursday morning hearing would not be necessary since there would be no question of the validity of the warrant being used to hold him in custody. The coroner chimed in with his opinion that any indictment would also negate his need to hold an inquest into Mary's death.

Bargeron must have been a good poker player, because he knew when to play his hand. Without fanfare, he presented his evidence the next day to the sitting grand jury, which deliberated for three hours before returning two indictments. The first was expected and had been rumored for days. Chester Burge was indicted for murdering his wife, and the count specifically alleged that he personally and physically killed her "with his hands, his fists, straps, bands, garrotes, tourniquets, and other instruments of like kind to the grand jurors unknown, the same being weapons which, as used by the said accused, were deadly and dangerous weapons likely to produce death . . . "

The second count, however, was shocking and caught everyone except police investigators by surprise. Chester was indicted for sodomy with his chauffeur, Louis. The newspaper account only went so far as to elaborate, with some delicacy, that Chester did "unlawfully have carnal knowledge and connection against the order of nature" with him. The indictment was even more specific, even if couched in legal terms, that Chester "by then and there taking into his, the said accused's, mouth the private male organ of the said Louis Roosevelt Johnson." Even though Johnson was waiting outside the jury room, he was never called to testify, nor was he indicted on any count.

Bargeron's quick and direct appeal to the grand jury was a wise one. Had the inquest scheduled for three days later actually been held, Chester's attorneys would have heard the evidence against him. Since a defendant and his attorneys are not present in a grand jury presentation, they still had no access to what evidence Bargeron held.

On the day after the indictments were handed down, John Burge personally appeared before the Court of Ordinary to present his mother's will in solemn form. He gave to Judge Walter C. Stevens, the same judge who had presided over the 1945 dispute over Clara Dunlap Badgley's will, a copy of his own letter of resignation from Auburn so that his residency in Bibb County would not be in question. The judge noted that John could have taught anywhere he wanted so long as his residence remained in Bibb County. Perhaps Chester pressed his son to take such a step. He knew what lay ahead of him and how little support he would have. For his part, perhaps John wanted to have personal stewardship over his own large inheritance. He knew just how much this expensive defense was going to cost. Charles Adams and Hank O'Neal already knew what was coming and had been adamant that they were representing Chester only on the murder charge. As for the sodomy indictment, he was on his own.

CHAPTER NINE

Every attorney wants to win. Think of a coach with his assembled team in a locker room about to begin a game. Of course he runs quickly through some important strategy, but at that point, if his players aren't physically prepared, they may as well not take the field. The vital role the coach assumes at such a critical moment is psychological. He must energize his team and appeal to their instincts for victory. The natural directive is to beat the other side.

Attorneys are no different. It is easy to imagine Bill West and his assistants, as well as Chief of Detectives Bargeron and the other police officers, as they prepared to go into battle against Chester Burge. In the crude language of the day, there was probably a great deal of talk about "the queer and the nigger." Surely twelve white men would do what had to be done to those two. And, just as a coach doesn't reveal his game plan to the other side, West and his team were determined not to reveal the cards in their hand.

Chester's attorneys scoffed at the sucker punch they were dealt by Bargeron. They saw the second indictment for sodomy exactly as what police intended—an effort to attack Burge's morals and reputation before the case ever came to trial. They immediately released the following statement: "The commitment hearing which we sought by a writ has been avoided by the maneuver of submitting the case to a grand jury where the claims of the prosecution cannot be tested." As to the sodomy count, the attorneys asserted, "Time will prove that the second charge placed by the prosecution was done solely for the purpose of fanning hatred and prejudice." The attorneys may not have planned to defend Chester on the sodomy charge, but there was no way they could ignore it.

The same day that Chester's indictments were announced, Mary's will was probated in solemn form, meaning that it could not be challenged through normal legal means. Chester's immediate inheritance was reported to be $129,000, and the judge of Ordinary Court announced that, unless the will were successfully contested, Chester would receive his inheritance regardless of the outcome of the charges facing him. His son, John, inherited the same amount as well as the house. The labyrinth of ownership concerning the numerous Mary Burge properties would take more time to navigate.* In reporting John's inheriting the house, the *Atlanta Constitution* referred to the "swank Burge home in fashionable Shirley Hills" as the newspaper made plans to cover the trial.

Solicitor General William West had disqualified himself in the Anjette Lyles case because of a distant relationship to the defendant. He was personally close to Chester's defense attorneys Adams and O'Neal, who were the prosecutors in the Lyles case, and Adams had worked for West as an assistant district attorney from 1952 to 1956. In fact, Adams named his son (now Judge William Adams) after West. The Burge case would eventually "strain" their relationship, but it survived intact and flourished, and the two families remained close over the years.

West had no intention of deliberately making Chester's defense attorneys angry, but neither would his friendship with them prevent what he had to do. Their public pronounce-

---

* In fact, in 2010 there are still properties owned by the family in Bibb County that were part of the estate.

ment that the charge of sodomy was a "maneuver" on his part brought this response from West: "Submitting the Burge murder case to the grand jury was not a 'maneuver' as charged by counsel for the defense, nor was the sodomy indictment returned by the grand jury 'solely for the purpose of fanning hatred and prejudice' against Chester Burge, as the lawyers have charged, but these indictments were returned because the evidence shows the guilt of these offenses . . . I do not wish to try the murder case or the sodomy case against Chester Burge in the newspapers, or through other news media, because obviously this would be unfair." West insisted that he wanted to try the case "only in the court room before a judge and jury where a calm, deliberate, fair, and impartial trial may be had."

The tit for tat continued, with the defense attorneys issuing a statement contending that the previously scheduled habeas corpus hearing set for later in the week should continue as planned since they believed that the indictments were based purely on hearsay. They contended that West should "be ready and willing to proceed with that hearing" if his assurances as to the indictments were correct. The defense attorneys were already earning their large fee by forcing West to do what he said he did not wish, to try the case in the media. Backed into a corner, West had little choice but to proceed with the hearing. But Chester's attorneys still would not hear what evidence the police and prosecutors were holding.

The only issue in question at the hearing was whether Chester was arrested properly and his rights properly protected. He had not been brought before a magistrate, as required within seventy-two hours if arrested without a warrant, or within forty-eight hours with a warrant. Chester attended the hearing, dressed in a business suit instead of the pajamas and robe to which everyone had become accustomed. His son, John, was absent. Arnold Jacobs, the only one of Chester's three attorneys who spoke, immediately contended that the presentment to the grand jury "circumvented" the process. Jacobs had to admit that his team "cannot now say that our effort to obtain a commitment has been circumvented" by the return of the murder indictment. The judge ordered immediately that papers be drawn up dismissing the writ of habeas corpus. Not one word of evidence had been presented. Chester was returned to his cell on the top floor of the Bibb County courthouse.

Macon Police received a mixed blessing with the announcement that Harry Harris had been assigned to the Burge case from the Bibb County Sheriff's office. Harris had been working for the sheriff since 1953, and his father was a deputy sheriff before him. He was well acquainted with attorneys Adams and O'Neal; he was the lead investigator in the Anjette Lyles case. His appointment, however, elicited some grousing from the police department, since it seemed to indicate that they were not up to the job. Solicitor General West, who specifically requested that the sheriff assign Harris, made certain to point out publicly that all the investigation upon which the indictments were made came from the work of Macon police, and that Detective Chief Bargeron was still in charge.

Harris worked for the sheriff's office for more than forty years and retained an amazing recall for cases when I interviewed him well after his retirement. Chester's was no exception. He said that the prosecution was "underrepresented" in the case and that Bill West asked for him because the solicitor general's office was "getting little cooperation out of the city." Harris would not make any pejorative statements about Macon police, but he did say "they were not bad but they were not efficient" and that "they weren't spending all the time on the case they should have." He did admit, however, that "it was easy to manipulate the police." His admiration for Adams and O'Neal was palpable, and he insisted that Chester had been "represented by the best" since "the case was tailor-made for those two."*

After being briefed on the investigation, Harris went to inspect the crime scene. In the previously locked closet, he found "lots of blankets all full of cash—one contained an estimated $50,000 in cash." Since this was long after Chester's arrest and a supposedly thorough examination of the bedroom by police, Harris wanted to know, "Why hadn't they confiscated it?" That discovery also raises the question of why Chester needed $41,000 from Mary to buy the Florida hotel if he had $50,000 in cash in the closet. Perhaps he wanted to sell some of their properties in order to raise the funds, or, even more likely, he was already being watched by the IRS and did not want to arouse further suspicion by the appearance of undisclosed cash with no legitimate evidence of how he acquired it.

Harris traveled to Auburn to meet with John and Jo-Lynn before their permanent move to Macon. He said that Jo-Lynn "was really nice. She and Chester didn't get along." He immediately recognized some tension in her relationship with John because he leaned toward his own family and "she just didn't know what kind of family she was getting into." Jo-Lynn's son

---

* In fact, the only reason that Harris, who is now deceased, agreed to meet with me was because I was accompanied by Charles Adams's grandson, Brian Adams, who was then a law student and now is an attorney.

recalls that, whenever Chester and Jo-Lynn would enter the same room, "the hair on the back of their neck would just bristle." Chester's attorneys reacted publicly to Harris's appointment with pleasure and the hope that "the true identity of the slayer" could now be discovered.

Immediately after the long July Fourth weekend, Chester's attorneys filed a mandamus petition, signed by their client, in Superior Court to force the inquest that had been cancelled after Chester's indictments. A mandamus is a writ under common law to force a public duty—in this case a coroner's inquest into Mary's death. The writ named the coroner as the defendant, asking that he be required to hold an inquest under Georgia's postmortem examination laws. A coroner's inquest is held when the coroner and perhaps the medical examiner cannot determine the "cause and manner" of death and a jury is convened to hear the medical evidence and reach a determination. The Superior Court judge, A. M. Anderson, was said to be examining the legal question of whether a subsequent indictment nullifies a requirement for an inquest. The coroner said that he definitely thought an inquest should be held, but "not being a lawyer," he didn't know whether the indictment cancelled his obligation under state law. He did admit that, prior to the indictments, police investigators had asked him to delay an inquest because they were not ready. Chester's attorneys, pressing the point, said they would appeal to a higher court if Judge Anderson denied their request. Finally, the legal gamble paid off and an inquest was scheduled for August 16, when the coroner agreed, even though the judge was still deliberating. More than three months after Mary's death, Chester and his attorneys would finally see what evidence was being held against him.

As Chester sat languishing in jail, John tried to take over the reins of the family businesses. Because of a cash crunch, it was necessary to sell some Burge real estate. In early August, a tract of land in the city's Pleasant Hill neighborhood on Woodliff Street, Monroe Street, and Fifth Avenue was sold to the Macon Housing Authority for $41,250. Perhaps there is some irony in the fact that land formerly owned by someone considered to be a slumlord was developed as a housing project named for Lewis H. Mounts, a respected black leader and former assistant principal of Ballard High School. Although Pleasant Hill, formerly a cohesive neighborhood of accomplished and proud black citizens, was almost destroyed by the construction of I-75 directly through its heart, the Mounts apartments still exist near the Booker T. Washington Center.

Finally, on August 16 Chester and his attorneys would hear the evidence against him. Although the judge had still not acted on their writ of mandamus, the coroner agreed on his own volition to hold the inquest. The long-delayed event was held in a courtroom at the Bibb Superior Court. In addition to the medical examiner and the doctor who first reached Mary's lifeless body, several police officers and investigators were subpoenaed to testify. Coroner Lester Chapman, who had agreed to the inquest after all, broke his leg the week before and was represented by a deputy, Adam H. Greene, because Chapman was still recuperating at Macon Hospital. Both Louis Roosevelt Johnson and the former chauffeur, Gene Robinson, as well as the maid, Jessie Mae Holland, and Chester's cousin, Olivia Kyle, were among those called to testify. The defense promised a vigorous cross-examination of the prosecution's witnesses.

A coroner's jury of five men was empanelled, and the prosecution introduced evidence of a "fresh" fingerprint found on the locked door that the killer had supposedly tried to open. Detective Marshall Pearce positively identified it as belonging to Chester. Mrs. Kyle was the next to take the stand. She testified that she was summoned by Jessie Mae and ran upstairs to Mary's bedroom. "Mrs. Burge was lying in the bed with her head bent over. We knew something was wrong without entering the room," she said. She also testified that "someone" called her a short time after the discovery and asked her to go to the hospital to tell Chester about the murder scene. She found him in his bed, although on the day before when she visited, Chester, whom she described as "a very good complainer," had been out of bed. He had found a hole in the mattress and was waiting for the new bedding he demanded.

Jessie Mae was next, and her testimony became the most crucial both in the coroner's inquest and the subsequent trial. She said she watched "for three or four minutes" on the day before the murder when the chauffeur, Louis, washed the door in question. Under cross-examination by the defense at the inquest, however, she said she only watched for "three or four seconds." She also noted that Mary's window shade in her bedroom was the only one closed in the house, and she noticed because it was highly unusual. Jessie Mae said that Louis came to her house about 9:00 p.m. the night of the murder but left shortly afterward. In an unusual admission that must have raised eyebrows, she said that Louis went home to his own wife then returned to Jessie Mae's shortly before midnight, staying until about 7:00 a.m. the next morning. She also disclosed that, shortly before she found Mary's body, a man who did bookkeeping for the Burges came to the front door to deliver some records but he did not enter the house.

Dr. Campbell, the medical examiner, testified that Mary had been strangled but he did not believe it was by "bare hands." He believed that something smooth had been tightened around her neck. There were obvious signs that Mary had fought to loosen the item that was used to kill her. Campbell said there were marks on Mary's head that appeared to have been made from another weapon, possibly a blackjack, but no weapon was found. He also found blood spots on the rug and bed, and the only other blood he found in the house was from the dead parrot, which died hours before Mary.

Officer Pearce, who identified Chester's fingerprint on the door, said there were two other palm prints in roughly the same area as the fingerprint but he could not identify them. They did not belong to Louis, the chauffeur, or to Gene, the former chauffeur. The only other identifiable print found in the bedroom was that of former City Councilman Russell Matthews, who had been in the bedroom the day before Chester entered the hospital and picked up Mary's loaded revolver to look at it. When Charles Adams pressed Pearce about whether there was anything else in the house, other than one fingerprint, to incriminate Chester, Pearce refused to answer on the instructions of Detective Chief Bargeron, replying that there were still items that had not been returned from the crime lab in Atlanta. Adams returned to the issue of why these items could not be presented at the inquest, and West answered, "They won't be sent here until the Solicitor General orders them, and I'm not going to do so." Adams responded that the defense attorneys had a right to know what evidence existed to implicate Chester. After presenting a photograph of the door in question with smudged prints, the prosecution rested its case.

The defense called Chief Detective Bargeron to the stand. He had stated publicly that he could prove Chester was in his house on the night of the murder. He insisted that the single fingerprint could only have been left by Chester the night of the murder because the door was washed clean the day before. He also conjectured that Chester had pushed up the hinge pins on the door in question to make it look like a robbery. Calling the double hernia operation "a minor repair on a former operation for hernia," he asserted, "I do not know the person or persons who carried him to the house or what type auto." West interrupted at that point and insisted that the defense was asking for "hearsay" from the witness. Adams responded, "I've never been to a hearing like this," and West answered, "I haven't either." The exchange between the men was later described as "testy." West charged, "It's strictly a fishing expedition on the part of the defense to elicit information." When Bargeron, sitting in the witness chair, attempted to ask Adams a question, the deputy coroner who was presiding interrupted, claiming that the procedure wasn't proper. Adams answered, "I surely don't mind answering questions here," and Bargeron retorted, "And I don't mind answering them if I can." Adams asked if Bargeron knew of anyone who actually saw Chester at his house that night, and he answered, "Not to my knowledge." Adams then said in exasperation, "Do you mean to tell this jury that without knowing who took him there, what type of vehicle was used, or how he left the hospital, all you have to prove he was in that house that night is one fingerprint?" Bargeron replied, "Don't you think that's enough?" and Adams snapped in reply, "No, I don't." Finally,

Adams asked the witness, "Do you think that one fingerprint in a man's house is enough to convict him for murder?" and Bargeron answered, "Yes, I do."

As the final defense witness, Chester was called to the stand. In an unsworn statement* Chester flatly stated to the jury, "On the night of the murder, I did not leave the Macon Hospital. I did not kill my wife, regardless of what you men may think." Chester said of the supposedly fresh fingerprint, "I purchased my house in 1948. Fingerprints should be everywhere in the house; I've lived there twenty-four hours a day."

Adams made a brief closing statement to the jury and ended by saying, "If a man is guilty of murder by virtue of his fingerprints being in his own home, then may God help us all." And that was it. Four and one-half hours after it began, the jury retired to deliberate. It took them just seventeen minutes to return their verdict: Mary Burge "came to her death by murder by strangulation at the hands of a party or parties unknown to this jury." The next day's *Telegraph* headline was two lines high: "Coroner's Jury Says Slayer Of Mrs. Burge 'Is Unknown.'" Even the *Atlanta Constitution*'s major story was headlined, Slayer Unknown, Burge Inquest Finds.

If the defense attorneys thought they were going to get a full disclosure of evidence, they were mistaken. As Solicitor General West stated of the items at the state crime lab, he was ordering that they be held "until ordered into court—and I'm not going to order them into court until the trial." Everything against Chester, it seemed at the inquest, depended on that one fingerprint. Surely the prosecution didn't plan to go to trial with nothing else? And, if so, what did they have? As

---

* This procedure is no longer allowed under Georgia law.

the *Macon News* asked in its lead sentence the following day, "Is one fingerprint on a door facing in a man's own residence enough to convict him of the murder of his wife?"

The defense and the prosecution agreed on one point—the decision had no legal effect. Chester was already under indictment. Using the inquest decision, however, his attorneys sought to have him released on bail. The petition they filed with the court noted that, "the evidence produced by the state was insufficient, as a matter of law, to support a conviction of murder," and that Burge "does believe that no other competent evidence exists upon which a conviction of homicide could be predicated." The bail hearing was set for August 30.

The same day the bail hearing was set, Chester's attorneys once again proved why they deserved their fee. They filed in Bibb Superior Court a subpoena *duces tecum,* seeking to force someone from the state crime laboratory to attend the bail hearing and produce the evidence they were holding, including "all records which relate to any fingerprints, palm prints, or other impressions" as well as reports "concerning any clothing including shoes, bathrobe, chauffeur's uniform, and any and all other clothing" that were sent to the laboratory. After the filing, Adams said publicly, "What is the state seeking to hide? If the state has other evidence, we have a right to know it. But it's going to be embarrassing for somebody if the state pretends there is other evidence and then can't produce it." Bill West's only public response was that he had not yet decided what action to take, but if any legal challenge were made to the filing, it would have to come from the State Crime Laboratory, which might question the "admissibility" of some of the items and reports in question.

While that question was simmering, an unexpected legal challenge to the earlier inquest was raised. Evidently Bargeron and the Macon police questioned whether the five jurors for the coroner's inquest were improperly chosen since they had not correctly been listed on the most recent grand jury lists as required by law. Even though the law had been in place since 1953, no one had bothered to abide strictly by it in the past. Defense attorney Hank O'Neal immediately responded, "If it's a new trial they want, we're ready." The solicitor general replied that any challenge to the jury list must necessarily have been made at the time of the inquest, and, as far as he was concerned, the entire issue was moot since Chester was under indictment anyway. Bibb County officials decided to let stand the precedent of previous jury selections for coroner's inquests and the challenge was dismissed.

August 30 was not a good day for Chester Burge. First, the morning newspaper announced that he had signed a property pledge for $200,000 to the IRS. It was secured as collateral against a debt he owed to the U.S. government for taxes from 1945 to 1955. The largest amount owed for any one year, according to the IRS, was $42,250.43 for 1950. What was not made public was that the full amount actually owed to the IRS was $342,312.67. Burge was forced to sign over twenty-three houses, two apartment buildings, an office building, and several vacant lots. It was pointed out that this was a civil matter unrelated to the indictments against him for murder and sodomy.

That same day his hearing was held to seek bail for his release. He was first called to the stand and testified that he never left his hospital room until after Mary's body was discovered. Interestingly, Solicitor General West did not cross-examine Chester, even though he was under oath. Louis the chauffeur was a surprise defense witness and testified that, while he used a damp cloth and Ajax to wash the closet door where Chester's fingerprint was later found, he could not be certain that he washed it completely or that he covered every spot. Johnson said he "washed it as best I could." The biggest disappointment for Chester and his lawyers was Judge Oscar Long's granting of a motion by the state's assistant attorney general to quash the motion for a subpoena *duces tecum*. Evidently the individual to be served the warrant at the state crime lab was away on military duty at the time it was delivered by registered mail, and he had never personally been served. The crime lab official was in court on another case while the Burge bail hearing was being held. Once again, the attorneys would not learn what evidence the state's crime lab had in its possession. What was worse, the judge denied the motion for bail and Chester was returned to his jail cell. His trial date was set for September 19.

Next came a flurry of maneuvers in four separate legal actions filed in Superior Court—a plea of abatement on the indictment for murder, a demurrer to the same indictment, a demand for an immediate trial, and, most important, a demand that the defense be allowed to examine the evidence being withheld from them. In the last action, a rule *nisi* petition, Judge Hal Bell set a September 9 hearing to determine why the state crime lab should not be forced to disclose the evidence. There was even an unsuccessful demand that the indictment be held "defective and void" because in one place it listed "Mary E. Burge" while in another it was "Mary A. Burge."

By September 9 the situation had become intolerable for both Chester and his attorneys. The prosecution entered his house, where a maid was on duty, ripped the closet door and frame from the wall, and took them into evidence. His attorneys immediately protested, calling the seizure "another attempt to keep the evidence from the defense" and a "complete abuse of police power." Within an hour of being informed, Chester collapsed in his jail cell and was taken to Macon Hospital, where he was reported to have suffered "a stroke or similar seizure." A quick examination discovered no evidence of a stroke, although he was said to be suffering from weakness in his left arm and the left side of his face, as well as difficulty talking (a trait he had certainly never exhibited before). While Chester recuperated in the hospital, his attorneys issued a statement that city detectives entered the Burge home "without any court order or authority whatsoever and without asking permission from the owner and at a time when the owner and his wife [John and Jo-Lynn] were away from home." Police responded by saying they "had permission" to do what they did but did not indicate the source. Charles Adams shot back, "Who can give permission to do an unlawful act?" John sought legal advice; not only had he not given his permission to enter the house, but he "had offered the door to defense counsel to be used as evidence." The defense attorneys had planned to have the door photographed in place that very day, choosing not to damage the house by removing the door.

As Chester remained in Macon Hospital, his attorneys arrived at Superior Court at the appointed hour to make their case seeking access to the evidence being denied them. Judge Hal Bell said a number of other cases needed to be heard first and told them to come back that afternoon. An attending psychiatrist who examined Chester released his report to the public that day, finding, "Patient alleges stroke, but is most likely suffering from hysteria. Says he cannot use left arm but uses arm when not aware." Evidently there were no questions of patient confidentiality.

That afternoon the attorneys—minus Chester—were back in court and again they were unsuccessful. The judge sided with the solicitor general, who stated to the court, "I have a duty to the public not to disclose evidence where an unscrupulous defendant might attempt to disprove it through witnesses or perjury or otherwise. A defendant who is innocent has nothing to fear from the truth." Hank O'Neal responded that he was seeking only the technical data from the crime lab, since "When these people pull all this scientific information on a defendant during the trial, after months of investigation, he has little chance to defend himself against it." O'Neal also objected to West's insinuation that "we'd try to do something dishonorable or scandalous . . . this was in bad taste and shouldn't be said." West assured the court he was not attempting to reflect badly on defense counsel.

Two days later Chester was released from Macon Hospital and returned to his cell. An unsigned letter, scrawled on notepaper with many underlinings and postmarked from nearby Talbotton, Georgia, arrived at the court for the three defense attorneys. It read, "Most of the public believe that the butler and chauffeur killed Mrs. Burge. Ask the butler why he scrubbed the door frames twice within a few days. Put this butler under a lie test. Sure Mr. Burge finger prints could be on anything in his own home."

With the trial just seventy-two hours away, suddenly the prosecution moved for an indefinite delay because of "new developments" requiring further investigation that could

"connect other persons with Chester A. Burge in the murder
. . ." Judge Oscar Long granted the motion for a continuance,
and Chester's attorneys responded by a public statement that,
"When this investigation is completed, the prosecution will
know what we have been telling them for over four months,
that Chester Burge was in the Macon Hospital when Mrs. Burge
was killed and we can prove it." Alas, the next term of court
was not scheduled until November 7. Until then, Chester would
just have to languish in jail. Despite a 1952 state law that had
recently forced the release of another man who was convicted
of the murder of his wife, Chester's lawyers still were unable to
have him released on bail pending the trial. The law provided
that, if more than two regular terms of court are convened and
adjourned after the term at which a demand for trial is filed and
the defendant is not given a trial, then he must be discharged
and acquitted. Obviously the law was elastic in dealing with
someone the police were determined to convict.

On Friday, October 7, both sides were represented at
court to set a definite date for trial. Despite repeated defense
demands for setting a date, West surprised Chester's attorneys
by arguing that, since four juries had been convened in the
prior several months and Chester's attorneys had not been
in court "ready for trial," they had forfeited his right to have
a jury trial. Evidently it didn't matter that those four juries
heard only civil matters and there had been no criminal cases
during those months. Flabbergasted, the defense attorneys
asked for a continuance in order to respond. Meanwhile, the
judge set November 7 for trial. His attorneys filed yet another
motion for bail.

Finally, all the attorneys seemed to reach what could not
be called a truce, but at least a stand-off. If the prosecution

would agree there would be no more delays in beginning the trial, the defense would stop pressing for bail. In late October, Chester was indicted once again, with exactly the same wording as before, but this time Mary's name was corrected in the one place that had been wrong. Both sides began completing forms to subpoena their witnesses and some of the names to be called appeared on both lists. Even Mrs. Ralph Gibbs, the mother-in-law of Macon Mayor Ed Wilson, was to be called to the stand. Although the two were not friends, Mrs. Gibbs was a Shirley Hills neighbor. She called Mary Burge only hours before the murder to tell her how sorry she was that the Ku Klux Klan had demonstrated at the Burge home two weeks previously.

While both the murder and sodomy counts were listed for trial, it was generally understood that the murder trial would be held first even though some of the witnesses would testify at both proceedings. Fingerprint witnesses were prepared to bolster the argument of each side. Because the defense had been stymied in learning what other evidence might be used by the prosecution, they could only be prepared on this one issue and hope to be able to handle anything else thrown their way.

On Monday, November 7, Chester Burge would finally emerge from six months in captivity to face his accusers. His attorneys knew they would be working hard to keep a hated man from the death sentence everyone expected.

CHAPTER TEN

Willard McEachern worked at the Bibb Supply Company when he was chosen to serve on the jury that would try Chester Burge for murder. Defense attorney Hank O'Neal looked over the list of prospective jurors and, seeing McEachern's name, knew that they shared a friend. O'Neal asked the friend whether McEachern would be able to render a vote of "not guilty" if the facts supported it and the friend said he would. When I visited McEachern and his wife at their home in 2003 (he is now deceased), he recalled the case clearly. He thought Chester's defense attorneys made a very wise choice early in the process. "They did a good job to begin with to make us aware that this was not a sterling character but he was not a murderer. He might be guilty of a lot of things but not murder." Chester's attorneys were not trying to make him popular. In fact, when McEachern said to me, "Well, I guess he was a queer," he lowered his voice to a whisper on the last word (which he delivered in the distinctive old Macon accent as "kwee-uh") in an apparent effort not to offend his wife, who was sitting next to him.

Eighty-four voters were called for the jury pool, and a great majority of them were men. Almost half had their names stricken with "cause" written as the reason. In a town like Macon, it was difficult not to know or have some type of relationship with Chester, his attorneys, the police, or the prosecutors. The first panel of forty-eight, followed by another of twenty-four, then a final one of twelve, were all asked qualifying questions before either side began their selections. Of that number, thirty-nine were stricken for cause, and twenty-seven of those were excused because they said they were opposed to capital punishment.* The state had every intention of asking that Chester be put to death and they weren't going to be stymied by conscientious objections. The other twelve said they already had a preconceived notion of the defendant's guilt or innocence. That left a pool of forty-five jurors available for questioning by each side. When the court broke for lunch, the clerk assured the judge he would have three more possible jurors qualified so that the prospective pool to be questioned in the afternoon would total forty-eight.

Hank O'Neal's quick and informal questioning of a mutual friend whether Willard McEachern could vote for an acquittal if the facts supported it indicates that the defense performed what little jury research was available to them at the time. In the afternoon session, Charles Adams asked each man or woman (there were only three of the latter) whether he or she could try Chester impartially even if his demeanor or personality was "obnoxious." The defense rejected thirteen prospective jurors and the state six; the remainder were dismissed. By 3:15 p.m., twelve men were empanelled and no alternates were named. The *Atlanta Journal* noted that seven of the twelve were "bespectacled, as is Burge." The jurors were warned not to listen to any television or radio reports nor could they read newspaper accounts or discuss the case with one another. The trial began immediately.

Juror Willard McEachern remembered a not-so-subtle attempt at showing public support for Chester. In the front row sitting as spectators were three or four ladies from the

---

* It is counterintuitive that one-third of prospective jurors in 1960 central Georgia were opposed to capital punishment.

respected Howard Community Club. They were sisters or family members of defense attorney Hank O'Neal.

Adams tackled head-on the subject of Chester's personality in his opening statement. He told the jury that the defendant "has personality traits that make him obnoxious, arrogant, moody, and difficult to understand," but insisted that he was not guilty of murder. All of them were aware of the impending sodomy trial, and the defense could not ignore that fact even if this jury would not be asked to consider that particular indictment. Adams maintained that Chester was on trial for murder because the police had been stymied in their attempt to arrest anyone else, and that this was the first major crime under a new organizational arrangement at the police department, so the desperate officers were attempting to "make the crime fit the person." He also admitted that, while Chester and Mary had enjoyed financial success, their marriage was not a happy one. In fact, he said, they and their family were "a strange tribe of people." Adams insisted that "pressure and prejudice" led police to charge Chester with his wife's murder. He pointed out that Mary and Chester operated their business from their home, and many "strange and unusual" people came there seeking to borrow money. Finally, Adams told the jury, "We believe that lack of evidence on the part of the state will result in bringing into evidence every weakness in this man's personality. But," he continued, "we can't be like Perry Mason. While the evidence will show Burge is not guilty, we cannot show who is." Adams also reminded the jury that the burden was on the state to prove Chester's guilt beyond a reasonable doubt.

Bill West, the solicitor general, insisted that the "feigned" robbery attempt the night of Mary's death was a clumsy attempt to trick police into thinking that was the motive for the murder. Although he did say that the prosecution would prove that Chester had been in his own house that night, there was no mention of an eyewitness to whom he had referred in earlier statements. If there was additional incriminating evidence he had been hiding all this time, he did not refer to it in his opening statement.

While Chester sat quietly in a brown business suit, occasionally whispering to his attorneys, the first witness called was E. G. Kyle, the husband of Chester's cousin, Olivia. The Kyles had been living temporarily in the guest house with their three children when they were summoned by the maid the morning of the murder. Kyle testified that he found Mary "lying on the bed—she'd been beaten and had a death look about her." He immediately called the family physician. Under cross-examination, he said that he did not hear anything out of the ordinary that night nor had he seen or heard any cars drive up to the house. Kyle did point out, however, that the windows in the cottage were closed and that the driveway was on the front of the house out of sight of the guest cottage.

Dr. Birdsong, who had first been called to the house, testified that it was obvious when he arrived Mary was dead. She had "marked discoloration" around her neck and face and "rigor mortis had set in." After confirming death, the doctor twice tried to call the police chief but was told he was "out ribbon-cutting" at a ceremony. He then told the radio sergeant about the murder and officers were dispatched immediately. After those two witnesses gave their testimony, the judge recessed until the following day.

Tuesday, November 8, was not only the second day of the Burge trial but also presidential election day. Special arrange-

The wealthy and powerful Samuel S. Dunlap family held one of Macon's few fortunes at the turn of the century. Their black sheep cousin, Chester Burge, was determined to get his hands on it. He finally saw his chance with Clara, the last one alive, seated here at far left next to her father. The older woman seated in front, Mrs. Samuel Dunlap, was born Mary Burge, a daughter of Chester's great-grandparents. Standing left to right: Lillian, Ilah, and Florine. Seated left to right: Clara, Captain Samuel Dunlap, Samuel, Jr., Mrs. Samuel Dunlap, and Nettie. *Courtesy of Jack Caldwell.*

The wealthiest Dunlap of them all was Ilah, who inherited a large fortune after the death of her first husband whom she married when she was twenty-one and he was sixty-six. She later married John D. Little, former Speaker of the Georgia House of Representatives. They are pictured here at her South Georgia plantation. Her large bequest built the University of Georgia library. *Courtesy of Hargrett Rare Book and Manuscript Library / University of Georgia Libraries.*

Anna Dickie Olesen was the first woman nominated to the U.S. Senate, by the Minnesota Democrats in 1922. She later helped kidnap her own granddaughter as a wife for Chester's son, John, but eventually regretted her decision and helped her escape. Although Anna was eighteen years older than he, she became Chester's last wife in 1961. *Courtesy Prints & Photographs Division, Library of Congress.*

Chester tried to mimic the way he thought the upper crust acted and usually got it wrong. Here he and Mary publicize their planned trip to Europe in the same year he hired a photographer to capture the guests at his annual Christmas party. *Courtesy of the Middle Georgia Archives, Washington Memorial Library, Macon, GA.*

Called "an ambitious redneck" by a contemporary, Chester filled his home with fine antiques and desperately tried to be accepted as a social leader. Chester's annual Christmas party was a brazen attempt to force his way into the upper echelons of society although his guests often laughed at his pretensions as they consumed his food and liquor. *Courtesy of the Middle Georgia Archives, Washington Memorial Library, Macon, GA.*

Chester was always careful to invite attractive young people to mingle with his older guests. More than one became aware that he wasn't seeking only friendship, and there were stories of assorted sexual liaisons arranged at his parties. *Courtesy of the Middle Georgia Archives, Washington Memorial Library, Macon, GA.*

When Mary was brutally murdered here, the Atlanta papers referred to the Burges' "lavishly-furnished" home in "fashionable Shirley Hills." Just weeks before Mary's murder, the Ku Klux Klan tried to burn a cross on the lawn. *Courtesy of the Middle Georgia Archives, Washington Memorial Library, Macon, GA.*

Chester found in the handsome young Fritz Phillips the kind of upper-crust background he so desperately craved. Chester planned to take Fritz to Europe and to live with him in Florida until Mary Burge objected. *Courtesy of Fritz Phillips.*

This portrait of Mary Burge, wearing her expensive diamond necklace, graced the front parlor of the home where she would be brutally murdered after visiting her husband in a local hospital. Her noisy pet parrot died only hours ahead of her. *Photo by Hank Griffin of Drinnon studio for the* Telegraph *(Macon).*

Chester was lying in his hospital bed when he heard on the radio that Mary had been murdered. He was brought home still in his pajamas and robe, which the public became used to seeing during the early days of the investigation. *Photo by Hank Griffin of Drinnon studio for the* Telegraph *(Macon).*

Chester had a double hernia operation and was given two doses of sedatives only minutes before he sneaked out of bed unseen to murder his wife, if the Macon police were to be believed. *Courtesy of the Middle Georgia Archives, Washington Memorial Library, Macon, GA.*

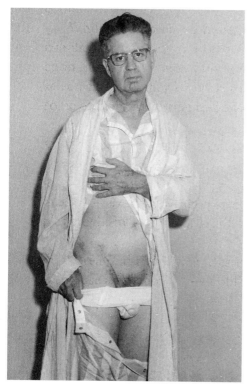

Even Chester's surgeon thought it highly unlikely he could have accomplished what the police alleged so soon after major surgery. His attorneys had this photo taken to support their defense. *Courtesy of the Middle Georgia Archives, Washington Memorial Library, Macon, GA.*

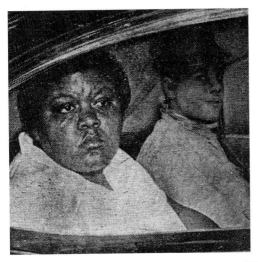

Louis Roosevelt Johnson (seen here with the maid who found Mary's body) came to work for Chester as a chauffeur and some-time butler, although his eventual duties often brought him to Chester's bedroom even while Chester's wife and mother were in the house. *Photo by Hank Griffin of Drinnon studio for the* Telegraph *(Macon).*

Olivia Kyle was a cousin of Chester's mother. She and her husband, who were staying with their children in the Burges' guest cottage at the time of the murder, both testified against Chester in his two trials. *Photo by Hank Griffin of Drinnon studio for the* Telegraph *(Macon).*

Chester Burge knew what he wanted and had no intention of letting anyone get in his way. As far as he was concerned, rules were meant for other people. Many agreed that he got what he deserved in the end. *Photo by Hank Griffin of Drinnon studio for the* Telegraph *(Macon).*

ments were made to allow the twelve jurors to go downstairs in the courthouse, accompanied by bailiffs, in order to vote. All of the jurors were white, so they voted on the main level while black voters were sent to the basement. As the tawdry business of murder and the underbelly of Macon were being exposed in a courtroom upstairs, voters downstairs were electing a handsome and dynamic young president who brought excitement and hope to a nation after the steadying yet somewhat dull hand of General Dwight D. Eisenhower (who flew to Georgia the day after election day to play golf at Augusta). Georgia gave 458,638 votes to Kennedy and 274,472 votes to Nixon* that day, a margin of 63 percent to 37 percent. In a then-record turnout of 24,910, or 78.5 percent of eligible voters, Macon and surrounding Bibb County gave 14,387 to Kennedy and 10,523 to Nixon, a margin of 58 percent to 42 percent. Election results were then still reported with different numbers for white and black voters. Only one Bibb precinct, a heavily white one in north Macon, went to the Republicans when both white and black votes were consolidated. In Chester's affluent precinct, which included Shirley Hills, Nixon won the white vote 647 to 592, but when black votes were added to those numbers, Kennedy barely won 702 to 696. Change was evident, and even wealthy white enclaves could no longer expect to guarantee election returns as they had in the past. Even today, Macon, now a majority-black city, remains a blue spot in the middle of an increasingly red state.

When testimony resumed, Louis took the stand to tell of washing the closet door in question. His account was some-

---

* Because Georgia voters actually had to vote for electors rather than the presidential candidate, by some counts Kennedy's margin in Georgia may have been approximately 1,800 less than reported here.

what changed from what he said in the coroner's inquest. The centerpiece of that day's trial was the door itself, set up as an exhibit in the courtroom. At one point, defense attorney Arnold Jacobs almost knocked it over, and at another, policeman B. C. Cranford had a difficult time opening it while trying to make his point that the hinge pins had been forced up. He said the top pin had been pushed up about five inches and the bottom one about three-fourths of an inch. Louis seemed to contradict himself from his earlier testimony, in which he had said he "went around" the door and might have missed some spots. This time he insisted that he had washed the entire door very well. His equivocation from his statements in the coroner's inquest appeared to have vanished. Even defense attorney O'Neal could not shake him. Perhaps police had, by this time, offered him immunity in the sodomy trial if he would testify against Chester. If so, they would have made it clear that he could not cast doubt on their single most important piece of evidence.

Dr. Leonard Campbell, the medical examiner, gave more details of Mary's fatal injuries. The ones suffered around her head might have been made by a human fist. She also had a bruise on her back, "brush burns" on her hands, and an injury to the knee. Her neck indicated she was strangled with "some constricting object," and there were other marks on her neck caused by her own fingernails as she struggled to loosen the object used to strangle her. He said the item used was "relatively soft and relatively smooth" because the skin wasn't broken.

The maid, Jessie Mae, testified that she had not noticed the condition of the hinges on the door that Louis washed. It was near the "jimmied" pin of the door that the supposedly "fresh" fingerprint of Chester was found. That fingerprint from the index finger of Chester's left hand was the crux of the prosecution's case, since they contended it could only have been placed there after Chester's operation and hospitalization, proving that he was at his home the night of the murder. Detective Frank Lanneau identified some of the photographs of both the murder scene and of Mary's injuries, including one which showed her hand "torn" in what appeared to be an effort to remove her diamond ring. He said that, on the day after the murder, Chester told him he had given Mary $5,000 in hundred-dollar bills that night at the hospital. Later Chester said the money was in denominations of three $1,000 bills and four $500 bills. The billfold found under Mary's mattress, where Chester told him to look, was the one Chester insisted he had given her that night, but it contained only one dollar bill and some papers. Lanneau testified that the door to the basement, where the family dog was found, was locked from the inside, and that there was "no sign of forced entry" into the house. The officer also stated that the new wills of both Chester and Mary were found on the bedside table and "the seal was broken" on Mary's but the seal on Chester's was intact.

A few other technical witnesses filled the remainder of the afternoon, although former City Councilman Russell Matthews did take the stand to explain that his prints on Mary's gun were placed there when he visited Chester on the day he was admitted to the hospital for his hernia operation. Matthews and contractor Louis Briggs had gone to the Burge home to discuss a possible construction project on some vacant lots owned by Chester.

Thursday's testimony was the most explosive of the trial and, in some ways, more damaging to Chester's reputation than his fingerprint on the closet door. First, photographs of the scene were identified. Then Chester's doctor, Milford Hatcher, testified. The prosecution had called the surgery performed by Dr. Hatcher "minor," strongly suggesting that he could easily have gotten up and left his hospital room. In fact Dr. Hatcher said patients are urged to get up and walk to help speed recovery. But Dr. Hatcher insisted that Chester's was major surgery, and on cross-examination, Charles Adams asked whether it would have been possible for Chester to have gotten up only thirty-six hours after a double hernia operation, under the effects of a double dose of sedatives, and made his way home and back again. Even more directly, he asked, "Could such a patient leave his room, drive a car across town . . . and lift a woman's body onto a bed thirty-nine inches high?" Dr. Hatcher replied that it was possible, "but unusual and not probable." He said the stitches from Chester's surgery might be strong enough to survive the efforts alleged by the prosecution "if a person could withstand the pain." Dr. Hatcher also testified that he went by to check on Chester the night of the murder between 9:30 and 10:00 and "I saw something in the bed; I couldn't say if it was Burge." Because he assumed the patient was sleeping, he did not enter the room. Dr. Hatcher also testified that, eight days after the hernia operation, he removed some moles from Chester's leg, toe, and back. Some bloodstains found on the lower part of his pajamas would most likely have come from that later procedure since Chester's pajamas and robe had not been confiscated for testing until afterwards. The state had entered into evidence Chester's much-worn maroon bathrobe in which he had been seen and photographed for more than a week after the murder. There was also blood found on his slippers worn during that time, but Dr. Hatcher again pointed out that it would have come from Chester's later surgical procedure.

A nurse's aide, Mrs. Jeanette Moore, testified that she bathed Chester the morning Mary's body was discovered. She found no scratches anywhere on his body nor any abrasions on his hands. This point was particularly important since Mary had fought her attacker violently and the prosecution contended, and the indictment stated, that Chester killed Mary himself. The medical examiner had already testified that Mary scratched her own throat while desperately trying to loosen the tourniquet from around her neck. It would be logical to assume that some scratches would have ended up on the murderer's hands unless he wore gloves, and evidence of gloves would weaken the prosecution's contention that Chester left a fingerprint that night.

Jessie Mae Holland was called back to the stand to testify. She said that Mary told her she picked up one of Chester's suits at the hospital to take it to the cleaners after removing a wallet from it. Supposedly this was the same wallet found underneath her mattress with papers and only one dollar in cash. Chester had maintained that there was $5,000 in it when Mary left the hospital.

John Burge next took the stand and discussed what must have been a difficult subject for a son at any time, and particularly in such a public venue—his father's relationship with Fritz. He said that Chester had expressed affection for the younger man and that the relationship between Chester and Mary became progressively worse once Fritz entered their lives. John said that his father had visited Fritz in Philadelphia on two occasions and that the pair planned to travel to Europe together. John also said that he had originally given his father the .38 revolver but later retrieved it and gave it to his mother for her own protection. Finally, he identified the diamond from his mother's large ring as well as codicils to both his parents' wills, which put each other back into place as beneficiaries and excluded outside inheritors. Evidently this step was taken after the argument when Mary found that Chester had made Fritz a beneficiary of his will and Mary had retaliated by removing Chester from her own. Finally, John said that both he and his mother opposed having Chester purchase the Florida hotel where he intended to live with Fritz.

It was the next witness, however, who garnered all the attention for the day. She was Sarah Burge Durden, Chester's mother and John's grandmother. And she was called by the prosecution as a witness for the state. This was the same woman who, as a young widow, went back to work to provide for her only living child. The same woman who had signed an order to have her son arrested and locked in the lunatic asylum. The same woman whom Chester asked to stay away from his home a few days longer yet failed to tell that he was being admitted for surgery. And the same woman who knew of her son's love for Fritz. Considering her sworn testimony, perhaps Sarah Durden could empathize with Shakespeare's words:

> Turn all her mother's pains and benefits
> To laughter and contempt; that she may feel
> How sharper than a serpent's tooth it is
> To have a thankless child!*

Mrs. Durden described her son as "mean," testified that he and his wife "fussed more or less continuously," said he often

---

* Shakespeare, *King Lear*, 1605; act 1, scene 4, 286–289

beat his wife, and on several occasions threatened to kill her. She said, since Fritz's first visit to the Burge home in October of 1959, Chester "was always throwing it up to her—that he loved Fritz more than he did her. It liked to have killed her." She also insisted that she had seen Chester kick Mary "until the blood ran down her leg." Mary ran into the house to get away from him on that occasion. Asked the reason for that argument, Mrs. Durden replied it was "over a frivolous thing—about a little dog." Because she lived with Chester and Mary, Mrs. Durden had an unusual opportunity to witness her son's brutal behavior. She said that she was particularly close to Mary, and several times she would hear her scream and run to Mary's door to see if she could help. On one occasion, Mary replied from behind her locked bedroom door, "Chester's in here beating me to make me do things I don't want to do," and that Chester had beaten Mary's head against the wall on more than one occasion. Finally, Mrs. Durden told of a conversation at home when Chester was planning to take the young high school student with him to Europe. Mary "thought it was wrong to take the boy off," said Mrs. Durden. All this testimony was given while her son sat only yards away from her; her grandson, having already finished his own testimony, sat in the courtroom as well. Even Chester's attorney, Charles Adams, could not get her to back down when he cross-examined her. Adams asked whether Chester "seemed to get any particular pleasure out of arguing," and Mrs. Durden replied that he did. When asked whether his moodiness seemed to come in phases, she answered that, since the previous October, when Fritz first came to visit, Chester had "seemed to be in a bad mood just about all the time." That afternoon newspaper's front page was headlined BURGE THREATENED TO KILL WIFE, HIS MOTHER TESTIFIES. The *Atlanta Journal* noted that Chester watched all the testimony "without a flicker of emotion" but busily scribbled notes on a legal pad, which he then passed to his attorneys.

Mrs. Durden's cousin, Olivia Kyle, took the stand after her and testified that Chester had wanted to buy the Lanier Hotel in Macon for Fritz to manage. When Mary wouldn't give him the money, he threatened to hit her with the telephone. Mrs. Kyle was asked why Mary had objected to the purchase and replied, "She didn't want him to give it to Fritz—she didn't think he deserved it." Mrs. Kyle was also present when Chester read Mary his own will, which cut her out completely and included Fritz as a beneficiary. Mary then changed her own will to exclude Chester. Mrs. Kyle admitted under cross-examination that she was aware that those codicils in their wills were later changed.* For the first time, Mrs. Kyle testified that Mary told Chester, in her presence, not to return to their home (which she owned) if he went on the trip to Europe with Fritz.

Mrs. Kyle told in detail about the trip that Chester and Fritz made to visit her in Tampa when Mary was later driven down by Louis to join them accompanied by Jessie Mae, the maid. It was during this trip that Chester found the hotel he planned to purchase and live in together with Fritz. Mrs. Kyle testified that Chester "told me several times that he was in love with Fritz." In fact, he said "he had left Mary and was not going back to Macon." Finally, Mrs. Kyle told once again about Mary's threat to expose Fritz to his family and friends in New Jersey. Chester responded, "Would you do that, Mary? Would you break up our friendship?" Mary's response was that she would not want "a friendship like that."

---

* Evidently the codicils were changed after the visit to Dr. Thigpen's office in Augusta when Fritz departed for his home in New Jersey.

Rees Smith, a microanalyst from the state crime lab, testified that blood had been found on Chester's "moccasins" and "lounging robe" that had become so familiar to observers. Two small spots of blood were found just above the sole on the right side of the right moccasin but, because tanning materials in shoes often give a false positive reading, no tests were run to determine whether it was human blood. The maroon and gray robe revealed two spots of blood, but tests could not determine whether it was human. Smith also found blood on Mary's sheets and pillowcases, but he could not determine the blood type. Finally, blood found on Mary's nightgown was A positive. Surprisingly, there was no evidence whether that was Mary's blood type.

When defense attorney Arnold Jacobs asked Smith whether the unidentified blood could have come from the dead parrot, he responded, "Yes, sir, it's possible." Hank O'Neal complained that police had waited "many days" to seize the robe and slippers. Chester's surgeon, Dr. Milford Hatcher, had already testified that it was possible the blood found on the robe could have come from the later surgery to remove moles on Chester's leg and back.

The state closed its case after four days of testimony without presenting any eyewitnesses who had seen Chester out of his bed that night. They had publicly contended as early as the coroner's inquest that they would present such a witness and that they would place Chester in his own home that night for as long as two hours. Now it was time for Chester's highly compensated attorneys to refute the state's case.

First, a civil engineer who had examined all the door hinge pins in Chester's house was called. He found that sixteen of them had worked themselves up like the one from the door brought into court by the prosecution. He also had measured the interior of the house and found that the sleeping porch where little John Lee was in bed the night his grandmother was murdered was only nineteen feet from the closet door, a distance that surely would have meant the boy would be awakened by someone beating on the hinge. Four nurses or nurse's aides then testified that Chester was given two doses of sedatives the night of the murder and was in his bed on several checks during the night. One even administered a shot of Demerol to the patient at 12:30 a.m.—and the murder took place between 11:00 p.m. and 1:00 a.m. according to medical testimony. She checked on him again between 1:00 a.m. and 2:00 a.m. and found him sleeping, although she did admit on cross-examination that, although there was a figure in his bed, she did not check to make sure that it was he. Another nurse's aide testified that she personally spoke with Chester at about 11:30 p.m. and at 12:20 a.m. There was additional testimony from nurses who bathed him and found him up out of his bed the day after surgery.

The assistant city engineer produced drawings of the hospital and had to admit that the only service elevator available to Chester was on another wing. He also agreed that, in order for Chester to have walked down the outside stairs, there would have been more than one hundred steps in each direction and the staircase would exit a door facing the hospital's main entrance, only eight feet from its circular driveway. Chester's hospital records were introduced into testimony, as well as a photograph of him taken after his arrest showing his surgery scar.* The star attraction—the appearance of Chester himself—was still to come.

---

* When I sent this revealing and explicit photograph to Fritz, even forty-nine years after it was taken, he replied, "I was surprised at my own reaction. RE-VULSION. I can't say that I thank you for that picture of old Burge."

CHAPTER ELEVEN

Finally, on the afternoon of Friday, November 11, came the witness everyone had been waiting to see. Chester took the stand himself to make an unsworn statement that would not subject him to cross-examination. He admitted that he and Mary had "never enjoyed complete marital happiness or the social prestige which we both wanted." He conceded that, during their thirty-six years of marriage, "We fussed and fought all the time. We found all of our common interest in business and financial matters." In light of his own mother's testimony, Chester said she was "very close to Mary" and that she "did not approve of our arguments." Still, he insisted, his mother could only offer opinions as she perceived them and "I know my mother has no malice in her heart toward me." Reacting to the state's contention that he killed his wife because she interfered with his private life, Chester insisted, "I had all the freedom I wanted—even to going to Europe without her." He asserted that he did not need to kill her in order to gain his independence.

Noting that a coroner's inquest jury had already found that Mary's murderer was unknown, Chester also reminded this jury that the prosecution had delayed his trial because they said they had strong evidence of others who were implicated in Mary's death. He was not surprised that police investigated him. As he put it, "they have their job to do." He insisted that "my habits and demeanor [became] more important to them than whether I murdered her." However, he contended that their only evidence against him, a fingerprint, was no evi-

dence of his guilt: "My prints ought to be there. I have lived
in that house for twelve years." He insisted that any incon-
sistencies in his statements to the police immediately after
the discovery of Mary's murder were due to "the shock of my
wife's death or the inability of the officers to quote me." He
had not wanted to give officers the combination to his home
safe because "we were already involved in tax matters."

The strain of the ordeal was evident as Chester broke into
sobs on the witness stand. Regaining his composure after a
few moments, he told the jury, "I do not know who killed my
wife or how she was killed. I was in the Macon Hospital and
did not leave the Macon Hospital. Her death was a greater
loss to me than to anyone else. I needed Mary more than she
needed me." He reminded them that he had been in jail since
May 20 and concluded, "There is nothing left to me but the
truth of this case. Whatever you may think of me, I am not
guilty of the murder of my wife, Mary."

If he and his attorneys thought he would have the last
word, he was mistaken. Solicitor General West rose to present diagrams of Macon Hospital to show how Chester could
have slipped out unnoticed and returned to his bed undetected. Defense attorney Arnold Jacobs objected strenuously, but
West argued that the evidence was offered to rebut the alibi
Chester gave in his unsworn statement that he had never left
his room. The judge agreed and the testimony was allowed.

Then it was time for both sides to give their summation to
the jury. After six months and thousands of dollars in costs to
both sides, it all came down to this moment. Solicitor General
West told the jurors that Chester strangled his wife with the aid
of an "accomplice" who had yet to be caught. For the first time,
the prosecution asserted that the unidentified palm print on the

closet door came from Chester's "cohort." "His accomplice will have a day in court," West argued, "but just because we don't have the other man, let's not turn Chester loose." He admitted he did not know how Chester traveled to his house and back, since the defendant was "the only man in this court who can tell us." He didn't know who the accomplice was, "but I know one man who was there. Let's administer justice to the one we know was there," he continued. West also said that Chester "could have walked out without being observed, and if he had been observed, what would anybody have thought about it?"

West argued that Chester's fingerprint, which he insisted could only have been placed there the night of the murder, was even better than "an eyewitness" because, while people may make mistakes in identifying someone, no two fingerprints are ever alike. When West argued that Chester killed Mary out of jealousy, revenge, "and perhaps one-half of her real estate income for life," defense attorney Arnold Jacobs jumped up to object, pointing out that Chester would forfeit all that income if convicted of murder. West insisted that there was a time period between 9:30 p.m. and 11:30 p.m. when no one positively identified Chester, and that would have been enough time for him to sneak out, go home, murder Mary, and return to his bed unseen. Even though the indictment insisted that Chester had personally murdered his wife, West asserted in his closing statement that Burge "had it done whether he did it himself or not." By law, he asserted, Chester was guilty of murder whether it was by his hands or those of an accomplice. Finally, West reminded the jurors of Chester's relationship with Fritz by declaring that he killed Mary "for his love and greed for money—his love and greed for lust," and for a "peculiar love—and a mighty dangerous love."

Chester's attorneys argued that it would have been easy for someone else who had access to the house to murder Mary while Chester lay in his hospital bed, insisting, "It could have been a real robbery." Charles Adams urged the jurors to put away their prejudices and not be swayed by evidence that Chester was "in love" with Fritz. "This is a trial for murder," he argued, "not a personality contest. If it were, we would be trodden down and beaten to our knees. We have no illusion about the personality traits of the defendant." He insisted that, if another "criminal act" was committed by the defendant, "then for God's sake let the courts punish him for that—not for murder." Adams reminded the jury that, while the Burges may have argued throughout their thirty-six-year marriage, they operated two businesses successfully together, one in his name and one in hers. "It wasn't his towel, my towel in the Burge home. It was his money, my money." The only freedom Chester did not enjoy, according to Adams, was "investment freedom" concerning their money.

Defense attorney Arnold Jacobs reminded the jury that the state had shown no possible means of transportation for Chester to have reached his house that night. "How was it?" Jacobs asked, "By helicopter? By taxicab?" Jacobs also offered any number of other possible killers, including the chauffeur, Louis, and the maid, Jessie Mae, as the most likely since they had complete access and could have taken the $5,000 Chester gave Mary that night. Going farther afield, Adams said that even E. G. Kyle could have slipped out of the guest cottage, murdered Mary, and returned unseen. Finally, he said that any one of the many "strange" people who came and went at the Burge house could have murdered Mary. Judge Oscar Long instructed the jury at 6:20 p.m. They went to dinner, and then at 8:15 p.m. retired to deliberate. At 11:12 that night, they sent a message that a verdict was not in sight and the judge ordered them put to bed until they would reconvene at 9:00 a.m. on Saturday.

Willard McEachern remembered being sequestered with the jury that night in a dormitory at the courthouse. In fact, his wife had to bring him an extra change of clothes. They were led by an able foreman of the jury, Herman Goetter, who was well spoken and patient. That evening, when they deliberated for three hours without reaching a verdict, "there were jurors on both sides" of Chester's guilt and "I think we took several votes," said McEachern. If they thought it was going to be a quick decision, they were wrong. They were going to be forced to debate the merits of the case.

The next morning they looked at the evidence that had been presented to them. McEachern thought the state "did a good job of fixing the distance and time it would have taken him to do it." Still, "We had serious doubts that he could have done all that in the time they said." While it was obvious that Chester was a bad man, the evidence presented by the police and prosecution just wasn't sufficient to convict him of murder. As McEachern recalls, "I was waiting for them to come present something else. They did not have enough to convict him."

Certainly Burge's legal team was superior. They carried through on their opening statement to the jury, insisting that Chester "might be guilty of a lot of things but not murder." As for the state's contention that he snuck out of bed that night and went home to murder Mary, "He would have been conspicuous going up and down the hall and the stairs," said McEachern. In the final analysis, he concluded, "I feel like he was responsible for it but couldn't have done it himself." The indictment charged that Chester had personally and by his own hands murdered Mary, but the prosecution's case did not support that claim. There was only one verdict possible under the circumstances.

So what happened to the witness who was going to confirm that Chester left the hospital that night? And how did he get back and forth to his house in Shirley Hills? The state spent a great deal of time and effort trying to answer those questions. Joe League, who had provided a loaner car from Huckabee Cadillac to Chester in the past, recalls, "When they were trying to prove that he did or did not leave the hospital and go home and kill Mary—of course I don't think he did, I think the black chauffeur did it—Chester didn't do it himself. It doesn't mean he wasn't capable of it, he certainly could have, but I don't think he did. I don't think he ever left the hospital. I had to testify that we did not loan him a car that night. That was a deposition. I was not in court, thank goodness."

At least one person swears that Chester was in his house the night of the murder and participated in killing Mary. Marianne [not her real name] is still an attractive woman and was obviously stunning in her day. She was at the time married to a very prominent member of the community but was having an affair with Leonard Campbell, the medical examiner, who was John Burge's close friend. When she first told me about weekends they all spent together in Atlanta, I asked her, "Was this in between your marriages?" She answered, "Oh, honey, we were all married, just not to one another." Through Leonard, she saw graphic photographs of the death scene and of Mary. She vividly recalls, "It was an awful, violent death. He [Chester] hired two hit men but he wanted to torture her first. He couldn't get up so he had her kneel down in front of him and he beat her." Those photographs were part of the official medical examiner's file and autopsy report taken home by Leonard Campbell, who planned to write a book about the Burge case.*

Erma Lanneau, whose husband was the first police officer on the scene, said, "There were fingerprints in the closet that didn't match anybody's. The police wanted Chester Burge so they didn't follow some leads when there were other possibilities. They wanted him." On another occasion when I visited her, she said, "It liked to have killed Frank when they lost that case. He only told me much later that Chester's fingerprints were all over the inside of that closet but the district attorney wouldn't get it entered in the testimony." It is instructive that she said "wouldn't" instead of "couldn't."

Harry Harris, the deputy sheriff assigned to assist police investigators in the case, recalled, "Law enforcement's assumption was that he went to the house and participated in the murder . . . We timed it and he could have done it." Jordan Massee, whose intimate knowledge of the entire affair was almost without error, recalled, "The story was he went with them but didn't personally strangle her."

Whether or not Chester was actually at his house that night, it would have been almost impossible for him physically to have murdered Mary and then placed her on her bed without assistance. Not only had he endured a double hernia operation, but he had a shot of Demerol and two sleeping tablets within

---

* His last wife refused to share those photographs or the official file. She asked for substantial compensation and refused what was offered as "not even in the right ballpark."

a half-hour of one another just before the murder. Who, then, physically killed Mary? Harry Harris recalled, "There were two guys from Miami who came up." The two stayed at the Holiday Inn on Riverside just off Spring Street where a close friend of Harris (whom Harris didn't want to identify) used to go for coffee. The friend overheard their conversation as well as a telephone call. Said Harris, "The two men moved into a room there while Chester was in the hospital. They were from the Jewel Box, a gay bar in Florida, and they had been summoned to do the killing, but Chester didn't come through with the money. He tried to fire them but they did it anyway." That account would certainly confirm the presence of two strangers who visited Chester at the hospital within minutes of Mary's departure the night she was killed. Police said early in the investigation that they had located and questioned the two visitors. Why were they not called during the trial?

What about the supposed eyewitness? Grocer and former city councilmember Rex Elder had many sources within the police department, and he recalls that Chief Detective Bargeron told him that Chester, or someone working for him, "bought the nurse [who was to testify that she saw him out of bed the night of the murder] a new Chevy and the nurse went to her doctor and got a statement that she had a nervous condition and could not testify" at the trial. Harry Harris agreed that a nurse saw him leaving that night. He said, "The nurse disappeared. Her sworn statement disappeared. She saw him going down the stairs and was concerned about him so soon after his operation when he was supposed to be careful."

Lisa Davis, the former Mercer University student who was on the periphery of Macon's lesbian community at the time, recalls, "I always heard that Shirley or Jo or both were on floor duty that night. If Shirley was the mystery witness, I'm sure she would've been happy to have a new car and money. Or maybe the prosecution was just blowing smoke." The names of Shirley and Jo certainly do not appear among those nurses or nursing aides who were called to testify. There is, however, the unnamed nurse who was working that night who quit soon afterwards. The hospital administrator testified that she had announced her intention to resign before the murder happened. Could it have been Shirley, and did she, in fact, help Chester in some way? That would explain why she announced her intention to leave even before the murder; she knew it was going to happen. At the very least, did she agree not to testify that she had seen him leaving the hospital?

The jury was reconvened at 9:00 a.m. Saturday morning. After some deliberations, Judge Long repeated his charge to them. Included was a clarification that, if convicted, Chester would forfeit his rights to his wife's money. He also added a new instruction that, while they were to consider the testimony of "doctors and others," including fingerprint experts, if they used a fingerprint to convict, it must be shown beyond a reasonable doubt to have been created at the time of the murder. Finally, he added a stipulation that they could reach a verdict of murder in the second degree if they found that the defendant did not personally murder the victim but caused the murder to happen. During the recharge, the *Macon News* noted that Chester "appeared more tense than earlier and listened intently to the judge during the charge, his face muscles twitching nervously at times." The judge told the jury they had three choices: guilty, which would mean death in the electric chair; guilty with a recommendation of mercy, which would mean life in prison; or not guilty. The jury went back to their work at 10:42 a.m. and, just twenty minutes later, they signaled by a light in the courtroom that they had reached a decision. They filed back into the courtroom and, shortly after 11:00 a.m., as Chester stood to hear his fate, he looked nervously around the courtroom for his son. Where was John? Why wasn't he there to support his father? Returning his attention to his impending fate, he heard the jury announce their verdict: "We the jury find the defendant not guilty."

Despite the prosecution's attempt to make the trial about Chester's character and his relationship with Fritz, the jury made the only decision they could under the circumstances. As juror Willard McEachern concluded, "It hadn't been proven. I tried to keep an open mind in spite of his activities and character. I didn't want to vote against him unless he was guilty. I just kept waiting for something else to fall." As the *Macon News* reported after the verdict, "While there were reports that other evidence was being held out and that additional investigation was being made, the fingerprint remained the biggest card in the state's deck at the trial. And the jury of twelve white men found it not enough." After the trial, defense attorney Charles Adams kept a framed slogan about the case on his office wall. His son, Judge Bill Adams, still has it. In view of the $50,000 retainer to dispute the evidence of one fingerprint on a door that may or may not have been properly washed, the slogan read, "Never before in the history of jurisprudence has so much been paid to so few to refute so little."

Chester was not immediately a free man after six months in jail. He was taken back to his cell because he still faced the sodomy charge, which Solicitor General West said would be tried at the next term of court. Chester conferred with his attorneys, then a professional bail bondsman was summoned for the $5,000 bond. Shortly afterward, John Burge arrived and Chester asked that he be allowed to sign instead in order to save the $275 bondsman's fee. The request was approved and the change made.

When John appeared, Chester asked him within hearing of waiting reporters, "Where were you up there?" John replied that he had been in "the hotel room" and had come as soon as he heard that the jury was returning. He missed the jury's verdict. Chester's mother was also not present. John explained that he and Jo-Lynn had stayed the night before until they heard the jury retired. Chester replied that he was "worried waiting up there" and did not want to call John. That was the reason he had arranged for the bail bondsman. After John's check was substituted, Chester thanked some fellow prisoners, his jailers, and several deputies, shaking hands all the way around. He then asked John, "Will you stay with me at the bus station until that bus leaves?" John answered affirmatively and drove his father in a "small station wagon" to the bus station. The house on Nottingham Drive was no longer Chester's home; it now belonged to John. Chester's grandson, John Lee, says that his father made it clear that Chester was no longer welcome at the house. In fact, John Lee never saw his grandfather again. Chester was going to stay with Fritz's wealthy aunt, Mrs. G. R. Cook, in Camden, South Carolina, but he would not be driven in his Cadillac. He would buy a ticket and sit on a bus just like everyone else. If he thought he was a free man, however, he was mistaken. As police officer Frank Lanneau said to his wife, Erma, after the verdict, "He's dead anyway."

CHAPTER TWELVE

Although Fritz never again saw or spoke with Chester once he left Macon during the police investigation, the same was not true of his family. When Chester boarded a bus, he was going to Camden to see Mrs. George Rae Cook, born Alice Lydia Hutchinson, who was a sister not only of Fritz's grandfather but also of Newbold Hutchinson, "Uncle New," who first introduced Fritz to Chester. She was called "Aunt Missy" in the family, and her husband, George, owned a very lucrative business in Trenton, New Jersey, that began with linoleum. As Fritz says of him, "Old George Cook was one of the richest men in a city of rich men." Fritz insists, within the Hutchinson family, "We were all very fond of each other but always lived totally separately [on the family farm]. We were the poor relations." The interconnected clan had decided to push young Fritz into the hotel business with Chester. As he recalls, "Aunt Missy joined Uncle New (Missy's brother) in boosting me into position. And in doing so became my pimps. As you can see, they didn't do a particularly good job of it." Because he deliberately shunned all things to do with Chester after his experience, Fritz did not keep in touch with that branch of his family. In fact, he says, "I hadn't heard that Mr. Burge hid out with Aunt Missy in Camden after the trial. Amazing; that put some color in her life, I'll bet."

While it may seem somewhat odd for Chester to have left town within minutes of his verdict of not guilty, he may well have wanted to escape not only the house where Mary was killed—which now belonged to his son—but also the knowing eyes of anyone in Macon. He would not have been able to walk down any street without being recognized and pointed out to everyone. Missy Cook offered the genteel lifestyle to which Chester aspired and, while a few of her friends might know of Chester's recent ordeal, at least a stranger at a cocktail party would not.

Even in South Carolina, however, Chester had to worry about his impending trial for sodomy—a charge that carried a ten-year prison sentence. First, he had no attorneys to represent him. Charles Adams and Hank O'Neal made it clear when they agreed to represent him at the murder trial that they would not touch the sodomy charge. Arnold Jacobs, the third defense attorney, told reporters that he had not been retained for that count either.

Meanwhile, the *Macon Telegraph* published an editorial titled Files Must Not Close On Local Murder Case. While admitting that "the jury reached the only verdict it reasonably could under the evidence presented by the state," the editors also made the point that "one of the questions most often asked now is why the defendant was held in jail so long before trial if the evidence against him consisted principally of one fingerprint on a door in his own home—even if the door had had a good scrubbing after he was hospitalized." The editorial urged the state to continue investigating the case and to find the person who committed "such a heinous crime." No one else was ever charged in the case, and it officially remains unsolved.

After only two weeks of freedom, Chester was back in Macon on December 5 to face the sodomy charge. Two days before trial, it was reported that Chester had conferred with several Macon attorneys, none of whom would represent him. Louis Roosevelt Johnson, the chauffeur, was still being held "on open charges" until the sodomy trial. Obviously, the prosecution had no intention of letting their only witness skip town. Police were humiliated by their loss in the murder trial and were determined that Chester would not escape justice. Chester returned as a guest at the house on Nottingham Drive where John and his family were now living. On the eve of the trial, a reporter reached John by telephone at the Burge house and was told that his father was not available. He also said that he was uncertain who would represent Chester in Superior Court the next day. John would not comment on a rumor that Chester was about to be hospitalized again.

That night, just after midnight, Chester was taken back to those familiar surroundings—Macon Hospital. He was examined by Dr. Z. S. Sikes, a psychiatrist, and Dr. W. D. Hazlehurst, a diagnostician. At 10:00 a.m. that Monday morning, instead of having Chester Burge standing in his courtroom, Judge Hal Bell saw John Burge in his father's stead. John explained that his father was in the Macon Hospital and asked for a continuance of the sodomy trial. He presented signed statements from both physicians confirming that Chester was in their care. Solicitor General Bill West immediately demanded a full investigation of facts, and the judge issued subpoenas for the two doctors.

They arrived swiftly and conferred with the judge in whispers so low that observers and reporters could not hear the conversation. Dr. Sikes told the judge that Chester had been under emotional stress for months and had lost thirty pounds since he was examined during the murder trial,* but he and Dr. Hazlehurst refused to say that Burge was unable physically to

---

* Evidently Dr. Sikes was the physician who administered "truth serum" to Chester and monitored his statements under the drugs.

withstand trial. The request for a continuance was denied, and Chester was ordered to appear in court for the sodomy charge to be called, in all likelihood, in two days' time when a current murder trial was to be completed. As John Burge left the courtroom, he confirmed that his father still had no attorney to represent him. He was reported to be scouring the courthouse to find someone. The next morning, attorneys W. O. Cooper and Ed Taylor met with the Burges to discuss the situation, although both stressed that they had not been hired. Cooper did say, however, that if he were to be retained, he would move for a continuance until January. Bill West said publicly that there had been plenty of time to secure an attorney, so he would vigorously oppose any effort to delay the trial. Chester was released from Macon Hospital that afternoon and went immediately to South Carolina, only to return to Macon the next day to meet with his prospective attorneys. On Wednesday, both W. O. Cooper and Ed Taylor agreed to represent Chester in the sodomy trial. Hank O'Neal, who had been his third defense attorney in the murder trial, agreed at the last moment to join the team, this time after being released from a written agreement with Charles Adams and Arnold Jacobs. Adams' son, Judge Bill Adams, surmises that O'Neal "was sufficiently intrigued with the technical legal defense available in the sodomy case." It was reported that Burge could not pay the fee demanded by the defense team from his murder trial to defend him this time on the sodomy charge, although Judge Bill Adams now says, "I guess at the payment of their price they would have turned up their noses and handled it."

"Turned up their noses" indeed. Among the historical Seven Deadly Sins, "lust" replaced "extravagance" when the latter term lost its sexual connotation. Lust is considered a sin in all three Abrahamic monotheistic religions (Christianity, Islam, Judaism) when it is pursued outside marriage. But, as the Bible itself and centuries of literature attest, there would have been no necessity for forbidding it if it didn't exist. Within the category of lust, however, sodomy and homosexuality have been almost universally considered abominations. The Old Testament book of Leviticus is particularly damning on the issue of sexual relations between men,* and the term "sodomy" owes its existence to that wicked city in the Bible.

In 1778 Thomas Jefferson authored a proposed Virginia law that would require castration for men who engage in sodomy. Perhaps surprisingly, it was rejected as too liberal since the law in Virginia at the time prescribed the death penalty for sodomy. Prior to 1962, after Chester was to be tried for sodomy, it was a felony in every state in the nation, punishable by lengthy incarceration with the strong possibility of hard labor. These were high stakes, and Chester knew that there was no way of finessing his way out of this one.

Finally, on Thursday, December 8, Chester's sodomy case began. His attorneys immediately moved for a continuance, alleging that Chester was "nearing the point of a complete nervous breakdown" and that the defense team had not been given sufficient time to prepare for trial. His attorneys claimed that a delay was "imperative to simple justice and humanity." Judge Oscar Long, the same judge who had presided over the murder trial, denied the motion, agreeing with Solicitor General West that there had been sufficient time to secure representation since the warrant was issued on May 20 and the indictment on June 6. Chester's attorneys then filed a demurrer to the indictment because it did not state the age of Louis

---

* Although New Testament scriptures offer a bit more compassion on the issue.

Roosevelt Johnson, and the applicable Georgia sodomy statutes called for different penalties according to the age of the
offender. That motion, too, was denied.

Prospective jurors began to be interrogated at 11:00 a.m.;
by the time of a 1:00 lunch recess, forty-four men had been
questioned. Of that number, ten were disqualified for cause
when they felt themselves unable to reach a fair judgment
because they were biased or prejudiced in the case. Interestingly, one of those stricken for cause was Quinton "Sandy"
Dent, the handsome young man who had been so desired by
Chester. Macon was, in many respects, a small town. He had
been an attendee at the Burges' parties on the arm of Shirley,
the nurse who reportedly was on duty on Chester's floor the
night of the murder. An additional fourteen jurors would have
to be qualified before the process of striking could begin.

The *Macon News* reported that, "Burge, who had appeared
calm all through his trial for murder last month, looked less
composed today and from time to time buried his head in his
hands between his knees. His son, John Lee Burge, who had
been called as a witness for the state in the murder trial for
the strangulation death of his mother, sat beside his father at
the defense counsel table." His public displays were not genuine according to several people who knew him. Hal Anderson
recalled that John "loved his mother. [If he sat holding Chester's hand during the trial] it was for a purpose. I'm not sure
what the purpose was, but it wasn't love. I don't have any idea
why." But Harry Harris had an explanation: "Good lawyer-
ing—he hated his father."

Judge Long was determined to move the case along swiftly. By late afternoon, a jury of eleven men and one woman
was chosen. She was Mrs. Eloise F. Helton, a widow who

owned the Bull Frog Café in Macon. Solicitor General West immediately began his opening remarks to the jury, informing them that Louis Roosevelt Johnson went to work for Chester in 1957 while on parole from Michigan, where he had been imprisoned for murder in the second degree. West claimed that Chester first proposed having "unnatural sex" with Louis in late 1957 and that those acts continued up until May 5, 1960, the date of the incident claimed in the indictment. West claimed that, when Louis resisted, Chester threatened to have his bail revoked. After that, the incidents occurred once or twice a week. Defense attorney W. O. Cooper told the jury that the charges were not true and the court was ready for its first witness.

Louis Roosevelt Johnson took the stand. The newspaper reporters did not relate his exact words in a more conservative 1960. It was sufficient to say that the "unnatural acts" were described in detail as to time, place, duration, and nature. Louis said that he would be ordered to wash up in the basement before reporting to Chester's bedroom. There, they would lock the bedroom door and Chester decreed that they not be disturbed. Mary and Chester's mother were often in the house at the times he described, and there could be no doubt that the two men were having sex. Even Solicitor General West did not take on the distasteful duty of questioning the witness but left that task to his deputy, Jack Gautier.*

----

* Gautier later became District Attorney and took his own life by shooting himself in the courthouse's evidence vault in 1972. He is one of four Bibb County district attorneys to have taken his own life while in office. A fifth died from injuries sustained when he was hit by a car, and a sixth was murdered when he chased some intruders from his girlfriend's apartment. Chief Detective Bargeron, who was so instrumental in the Burge case, was later hanged. Although it was assumed he took his own life, there was some question as he had allegedly been "involved in rackets with the Dixie mafia."

Johnson testified that he went to work for Chester in 1957 at the suggestion of his parole officer, Don Walters, who took him to meet Burge the first time. Johnson moved into a basement apartment in the house and each night would report to Chester's bedroom upstairs to be given his directions for the next day's work. It was shortly before Christmas of 1957, Johnson stated, that Chester first proposed their having sex. After it happened, alleged Johnson, Chester told him "all he had to do was pick up the telephone" in order to have Johnson's parole revoked. "I can break your back anytime I want to," Chester told Johnson.

When asked why he allowed the sex to go on for more than two years, Johnson said he did not want to have his parole revoked. On two occasions Chester actually took him to the parole officer. The first time Johnson waited outside the office while Burge spoke with Walters. On the second occasion, after the two spoke in private, Johnson was called in and advised by the parole officer to stop "fooling around" with the maid and to be in his basement apartment by 10:00 every night.

On cross-examination Johnson explained that he had been imprisoned back in 1948 because a woman he was "courting" at the time "hemmed in" Johnson at her house between a wall and a hot stove. When she threatened him with a knife, he hit her in the head with a stick of wood and she died two days later. Johnson said he could not remember the topic of their argument. In the closing minutes of Johnson's testimony, he made an important retraction. He had already testified that Chester had threatened him at least twice with having his parole revoked if he did not agree to continue having sex. But, under Cooper's cross-examination, Johnson was forced to admit that he had earlier told attorney Hank O'Neal during the murder trial that there was only one threat and it occurred when he first went to work for Chester. It never happened again. At that point Judge Long recessed until the following morning.

It was obvious by this time that Johnson was cooperating with police in all Burge-related matters. In the original coroner's inquest, he said he had not done a good job washing the door where Chester's fingerprint was found, while by the murder trial he insisted that he had. Perhaps having been locked up all those months without being charged was sufficient to make his testimony reliable to the prosecution. Chester's defense attorneys in the murder trial theorized in their summation that Johnson and the maid might have been the murderers, so any cooperation between Chester and his former lover was by then history. It is certainly logical to assume that Johnson had been offered immunity as he was never charged with any crime.

When court resumed the next morning at 9:30, fireworks flew when the first witness was called. He was Gene Robinson, the former chauffeur who had also been held in jail "on open charges" soon after the murder. Again, Assistant Solicitor General Jack Gautier was given the task of questioning the witness. He had just asked his first question concerning "unnatural sex proposals" by Chester when defense attorney Cooper jumped up to object. The jury was sent out of the room while the attorneys presented their arguments.

Cooper objected that the only sex acts or proposals alleged were those in the indictment and that it was improper to bring in allegations of others. He first asked that the testimony be stricken from the record. When that request was denied, he moved for a mistrial on the grounds that the evidence concerned an offense other than the one alleged. He said that the Robinson allegations introduced the issue of the defendant's character, which was not on trial, and that they were prejudicial, immaterial, and irrelevant. Defense attorney O'Neal cited several cases in support of their position, but Gautier argued that the evidence was being introduced to show motive and general conduct. Both the motion to strike and the motion for a mistrial were overruled.

When the jury was returned to the courtroom and questioning resumed, Robinson said that, the previous January, Chester called him to his bedroom and propositioned him sexually. Robinson refused and went out into the hall where he told Mary Burge what had happened. She "merely laughed," Robinson insisted. The second time Chester propositioned him, said Robinson, was during a trip to Tampa to visit the Kyles. On cross-examination, Cooper painstakingly took Robinson through months of dates when he had been alone with Chester, yet there had been no sexual advances. When Judge Long admonished Cooper not to try the patience of the court, he answered, "I'm entitled to a thorough and searching examination of this hostile witness." When Cooper asked why Robinson never told police about these supposed sexual advances during the lengthy time he was held in jail before the murder trial, Robinson said he finally did so after being held for more than six weeks. At that point, Cooper leaned into the table where the prosecutors sat and said loudly, "When—when did you tell these distinguished gentlemen all this?" Solicitor General West looked around him and said to the judge, "I think we could do better without his shouting in our faces." Cooper took an elaborate bow and said to West, "I most humbly apologize, sir."

At the same time the sodomy trial was taking center stage, John and Jo-Lynn Burge suddenly were in the news. E. G. Kyle, the husband of Chester's cousin, Olivia, who had been summoned the morning Mary's body was discovered, was scheduled to testify. The prosecutors learned that John and Jo-Lynn contacted him concerning his testimony. The two were ordered to appear in Judge Long's chambers, where he issued a contempt citation naming them for attempting to intimidate and persuade a witness not to testify. The solicitor general had filed the citation against John and Jo-Lynn, and Judge Long ordered them to appear in his court at 2:30 p.m. on Friday, the second day of his father's trial. They came with their attorney, Reese Watkins, who said he needed more time as he had only been retained one hour earlier.

The citation charged that, on Tuesday and Thursday of that week, John and Jo-Lynn tried to pressure E. G. Kyle about his testimony. The citation alleged they called Kyle's wife and told her that "it would be bad for Kyle if he testified and that if he testified it would only increase the antipathy between the Kyles and the Burges . . . and that Kyle did not have to testify and the court could not make him testify." In the Thursday call to Mrs. Kyle, the citation alleged, she was told her husband had "no business in Macon" and that John Burge had already "spent $32,000 in this case and that they were going to throw this case out and impeach Louis Johnson's testimony and that Mr. Kyle did not have to testify." That same day they supposedly called E. G. Kyle at the Bibb County courthouse and told him "if Chester Burge is convicted it will only cost John Burge money." The calls were made, according to the citation, "to intimidate and influence and impede and persuade the said witness for the state, E. G. Kyle, not to testify" as part of an attempt "to impede and obstruct the lawful and legal administration of justice." The judge granted Watkins's request for a delay in responding to the contempt citation. Meanwhile E. G. Kyle testified that, he, too, had been sexually propositioned by Chester twice but spurned his advances.

If, as others have contended, John did hate his father, why would he go to such elaborate attempts to prevent further damaging testimony? Perhaps the reason was financial and not filial. Two of the calls mentioned the amounts of money the legal process was costing John. There had already been an effective defense in the murder trial that cost $50,000, and the IRS was breathing down the necks of the entire Burge family. It would be logical to assume that John could foresee further legal appeals if Chester were convicted of the sodomy charge and was thus trying to cut his losses. Two days later, John and Jo-Lynn were back before Judge Long on their contempt charge, accompanied by their attorney. They admitted they were "technically guilty" and were each fined $100. Through their attorney they apologized to the judge before he set their fine. Judge Long said he could understand the feelings of John and Jo-Lynn and was "going to deal with them as leniently as possible." He said he was "sure they are genuinely sorry for what they have done."

The same Monday as the contempt hearing, Chester's sodomy trial resumed. Exactly one month to the day from his "not guilty" verdict in the murder trial, Chester entered the same courtroom and sat in front of the same judge. Detective Chief Bargeron, who had been so instrumental in the murder trial, took the stand. He said that in response to a question early in the murder investigation, Chester admitted to him that he was homosexual. When Bargeron asked how long he had known about these tendencies, Chester answered "all my life" as far as he knew. When Cooper cross-examined for the defense, Bargeron became unclear in his memory of when and at what point various witnesses in the murder trial might have been dismissed as suspects in order to testify for the state in the sodomy case. He had to admit that none of the witnesses had ever made a complaint about Chester prior to their being questioned in the murder case. The clear implication was that Johnson, Robinson, and Kyle had all been early suspects in the murder case, that none had ever made complaints about Chester before, and yet here they were testifying for the state on the sodomy count.

On the last day of trial, Chester took the stand to offer another unsworn statement, which could not be cross-examined. He insisted he was innocent of the charges and merely "the victim of persecution and perjury." He said of the witnesses against him, "They have sworn falsely against me." Chester testified, "I have been unduly persecuted. I have lost my property. I have lost my home." He made a new disclosure that he was "in the last stages of tuberculosis" and asked that the jurors free him, as "I am innocent of these charges." Then, with no witnesses called for the defense, it was time for closing arguments.

Defense attorney Edward Taylor began with a reminder that Chester was only charged with one count of sodomy, alleged to have occurred on May 5, 1960, with Louis Roosevelt Johnson. While he denied that it took place, he asserted, "If it ever happened, Johnson was an accomplice—equally guilty of a crime." He pointed out that any evidence that Johnson acted under duress was meager and unconvincing and that there was no allegation that he was "under threat of life or limb" as required by the applicable legal precedents. If Johnson was an accomplice to the sodomy charge against Burge, said Taylor, the law required that there be independent corroborating testimony from someone other than the accomplice, and none had been presented.

Assistant Solicitor General Gautier countered by citing at least one legal precedent that would leave it up to the jury's discretion to decide whether there was sufficient coercion to "destroy the free will" of a person taking part in such an illegal act as sodomy. He also mentioned that sexual offenses usually allow for several exceptions to such rules. Solicitor General Bill West summed up for the prosecution, alleging that Johnson "was in virtual peonage to Chester Burge." West stated, "For some reason known only to him, Chester Burge saw fit to have three parolees in his employ. Sometimes I feel that to take advantage of a person who is helpless is far more contemptible than to take advantage of a free agent." West reminded them that in Chester's unsworn statement, he "tried to create sympathy [and] avoided the facts—he couldn't face them." Whether or not Johnson was an accomplice in the case, West concluded, it was up to the jury to sort out "this sordid mess." He told them that Chester was "a cancer on society" who should be given the maximum ten-year prison sentence.

Defense attorney W. O. Cooper's summation was far more philosophical, filled with literary allusions and appeals for compassion. He began, though, by appealing to a far more base instinct, insisting that the prosecution's case was based on "a gang of niggers." The one white witness, E. G. Kyle, Cooper called an "ingrate" for having accepted Chester's hospitality so long before turning on him. Cooper asked why none of the witnesses had ever said a word against Chester before they were questioned in the murder trial.

Holding his Bible aloft, Cooper reminded jurors of the story of Christ and the woman caught in adultery. "You can take all the law books," he said, "but leave me the holy book and I'll go on practicing law." He quoted passages from Deuteronomy about slander and, from James 3:8, "But the tongue no man can tame; it is unruly, evil and full of deadly poison." Cooper quoted a speech by the nineteenth-century agnostic Robert Ingersoll contrasting Napoleon I with a woman who "would rather have been a French peasant and worn wooden shoes" than to push love from her heart. He listed famous homosexuals from history, including Julius Caesar, Alexander the Great, Virgil, Michelangelo, Lord Bacon*, Oscar Wilde, and the poetess Sappho. "How cruel, how mean can we get in laughing at afflictions?" he asked. "Homosexuals have a hereditary condition over which they have no control—it is as if a person had been born an idiot."

Cooper reminded the jurors that Georgia had no institutions for the treatment of homosexuality and that instead of sending Chester to prison he should be assigned to "an institution we haven't got." He begged them to treat Chester with compassion. Burge, he said, "has only one thing left under God's shining sun, a few years with the terrible affliction of tuberculosis." He insisted that "the State of Georgia has accomplished enough. He [Chester] lies prone and helpless upon the ground." The jury had already heard testimony that

---

* More correctly, Francis Bacon (1561–1626), Baron Verulam, and Viscount St. Alban, who was attorney general and lord chancellor of England. He seems to have been conflicted about his sexual preferences. He married late in life, having written, "A bachelor's life is a fine breakfast, a flat lunch, and a miserable dinner."

Chester's wife and mother were in the house when he had sex with Louis, and Cooper wanted to ensure the jurors were aware that Chester's humiliation was complete.

Then, at 4:50 p.m., the jury retired. They deliberated less than an hour before reaching a verdict. Chester and his attorneys knew that a swift decision was not a good sign. As Dr. Herman Westmoreland later recounted, "The court being as redneck as it was had to convict him of something" after not being able to convict him of murdering his wife. Judge Long called Chester to stand. With justifiable trepidation, Chester did and heard the jury's verdict—guilty—as well as their recommendation of no less than five and no more than ten years in prison. The defendant was reported to have taken the announcement "calmly." Defense attorneys immediately moved for a new trial, and Judge Long scheduled a hearing on the matter for 10:00 a.m. on January 24. A separate hearing was scheduled for the next day at 10:00 a.m. to set bail pending the January date. Until then, Chester would be returned to his cell. Solicitor General West said he had "grave concerns" about releasing Chester on bail "in a case of this nature." He thought the defendant should stay in jail until all his appeals had been exhausted.

At the next day's hearing to determine what, if any, bail amount would be set, Cooper set out his request that an ill Chester be freed until the January hearing. Judge Long asked whether he thought hospitalization was necessary, and Cooper responded, "Please, Your Honor, I am not a doctor." He did say, however, that Chester needed rest and perhaps medical care. Judge Long made a reference to the tuberculosis supposedly suffered by the prisoner, and Cooper replied that he was unaware of it until Chester's unsworn statement in the courtroom. During that discussion, John Burge rose and addressed the court. He said that his father had suffered from the disease for thirty years. He also stated that his father's nervous and emotional condition had worsened over the events of the past several months. Judge Long did not want Chester to be imprisoned until the January hearing if it would endanger his health, and instructed the defense attorneys to have Chester's doctors examine him and present a written report to the court. Until then he would not rule on the request for bail. Chester was returned to jail.

Finally on Friday, three days after the guilty verdict, the medical report was presented to Judge Long, although he did not release it publicly. Defense attorney Cooper said that, rather than going into a hospital, Chester would probably retreat to someplace quiet to "rest" if released on bail. The judge set a bail amount of $10,000, and John Burge signed the bond. Chester walked out a free man until his hearing for a new trial on January 24, the week that newly elected President John F. Kennedy would be inaugurated.

That hearing was delayed until Friday, February 3, when Judge Oscar Long again had the familiar group in front of him. The opposing attorneys presented their arguments supported by legal precedents and obscure points of law. Two hours into the hearing, Judge Long halted the proceedings and said he would reconvene the following Friday when he would continue consideration of the request. On February 10, arguments by both sides were completed in two hours, then Judge Long announced he would take the matter under advisement and announce a decision later.

Judge Bill Adams recalls recognizing the handwriting of Hank O'Neal on some of the written requests the attorneys gave to the judge to ask that he include in his "charge," or instructions, to the jury in the sodomy trial. O'Neal was obviously intrigued by the questions of law in the case, and, as Adams recalls, the court filings raising the ultimate defense "were mostly the handiwork of Mr. O'Neal." While O'Neal worked the appeals process along its tortuous path, Chester retreated to Camden, South Carolina, to the home of Fritz's great-aunt, Missy Cook. He was looking for something more than rest. And he found it.

CHAPTER THIRTEEN

Back in 1951, when Chester tried to import from Germany a Jewish couple recruited by the Lutheran church as his live-in servants, the contract they signed in the office of his fashionable attorney, Bill Turpin, was witnessed by Peter Olesen, a professor of German at Mercer University. Olesen was born in Denmark on April 20, 1879, then worked as a hospital orderly during the Spanish-American War. He immigrated to the United States, where he worked his way through Hamline University by selling books among a large contingent of Scandinavian Americans throughout the Dakotas and Minnesota. While passing through the village of Waterville, Minnesota, Olesen met a man named Peter Dickie, who asked him to come to dinner at the Dickie house. Olesen was struck by Dickie's only daughter, Anna, who was born on July 3, 1885, in Cordova Township, Le Sueur County, Minnesota. Anna had been a great lover of books as a child and was an orator from an early age. When she was twelve, her parents hired a speech coach to help her hone her prodigious oratorical skills. Anna viewed the wealthy summer residents of Waterville, who even supported a seasonal opera company, with envy and was determined not to end her days in small-town Minnesota. She would wildly exceed her own expectations.[*]

After obtaining what few educational opportunities were available to her, Anna became a teacher and lived at home with

---

[*] An informative account of the life and career of Anna Dickie Olesen can be found in *Women of Minnesota*, edited by Barbara Stuhler and Gretchen Kreuter, Minnesota Historical Society Press, St. Paul, 1998.

her family. When she met young Peter Olesen, she impressed him with her intellect and passion for literature. The two were married on June 8, 1905, when Anna was almost twenty. At the time, Chester Burge, whose life would become intertwined with her own, had yet to reach his second birthday.

The young Olesen couple moved to St. Paul, where they lived a Spartan existence while Peter earned his master's degree. During the time he was superintendent of schools in tiny Pine City, Minnesota, their daughter, Mary Winifred, was born in 1906. Two years later the Olesens moved to Cloquet, in northern Minnesota, where Anna finally came into her own. While Peter was superintendent of schools, Anna became active in Democratic politics. What little money they could scrape together was wasted on Peter's get-rich-quick schemes, and Anna longed even more for material success. She became active in the budding women's suffrage movement, recalling her grandmother's admonition that in the Civil War her husband had gone off to fight and afterward the vote was given to Negroes but not to her.

Anna began to rise in the Federation of Women's Clubs and was elected a delegate to the International Child Welfare Conference in Washington, DC, in 1913. Her fiery speeches on behalf of women's suffrage attracted so much attention that she was invited onto the national circuit and convinced Peter to hire a maid to handle her home chores and to care for their daughter. Their budget was still strained, however, so Anna decided in 1918 to travel with her daughter to Libertyville, Illinois, to audition for the Tent Chautauqua, a traveling group of orators who were paid for their services. She was successful and immediately began a lucrative career with the organization that would span a decade. Anna became a friend of

William Jennings Bryan, who was of great assistance in supporting both her oratorical and her political careers.

Anna Dickie Olesen became the first woman asked to speak to the Democratic National Party's Jackson Day banquet in Washington, DC, in 1920. National newspapers took note, including the *Chicago Evening American,* which wrote of her, "I saw in the lines of her face a great purpose. Her clear, bluish-grey eyes looked right into you—unafraid." Her success there brought immediate invitations, including one from the doyenne of woman suffragists, Carrie Chapman Catt, who asked her to speak to a banquet at the National Woman Suffrage Association in Chicago. Within months Anna was elected a delegate to the national Democratic convention to be held in San Francisco. The *Minneapolis Journal* printed her photo on page one with a mistaken story that she was to be nominated for vice president on the Democratic ticket.

In San Francisco, Anna was a floor leader for the campaign of Woodrow Wilson's son-in-law, the Georgia-born William Gibbs McAdoo.* Even though he lost the nomination, McAdoo led the voting on the first ballot at the convention. Anna endorsed a plank supporting Prohibition and, after being introduced by William Jennings Bryan, spoke in favor of it before the entire convention. After forty-four ballots, James M. Cox, the anti-Prohibition candidate, won the nomination. Anna won admiration from party stalwarts by announcing that she would support him and his running mate, Franklin D. Roosevelt, despite her efforts on behalf of McAdoo. In the fall Anna was asked to go on the road to assist in the vice

---

* Woodrow Wilson's first wife and the mother of his daughters was Ellen Axson, born in Savannah, the daughter of a Presbyterian minister. They were married in Savannah in 1885. She died at the White House as First Lady in 1914 and is buried in Rome, Georgia.

presidential campaign of FDR. Although Republican Warren G. Harding won the election, Anna continued her campaign in support of the League of Nations and won even more appreciation for her loyalty within the Democratic Party. Finally, in August of 1920, women won the right to vote.

Minnesota's incumbent Republican U.S. Senator, Frank Kellogg, was up for reelection in 1922. He had voted in favor of seating Michigan's U.S. Senator, Truman H. Newberry, despite his having been charged with violation of election laws. Anna relied upon that vote in deciding to seek the nomination of her party. According to one account, when Senator Kellogg was asked in Washington why he did not return to Minnesota to campaign, he answered, "I've got some Swede woman running against me." The other person replied, "That's no Swede woman, that is a Welsh woman and the devil rides her tongue. You'd better go back to Minnesota."

To the surprise of many, she garnered 28,745 votes, easily outpolling her two male opponents and winning the 1922 Democratic nomination. Anna Dickie Olesen became the first woman in the United States to be nominated to the U.S. Senate by a major political party. Barely stopping to rest, she went on the road again in the general campaign for the Senate, telling reporters, "I ask no consideration because I am a woman. I also ask that no one close his mind against me because I am a woman." She told the *New York Times* the night she won the nomination, "A man takes part in civic affairs without neglecting his vocation, and a woman can as readily adjust herself to the new order that is sure to accompany the new advent of women in politics." The *Gettysburg Times* of July 19, 1922, reported Anna's campaign story in a juxtaposition that must have been typical. Above the story is Anna's own campaign platform and ideals, ending with her statement, "First and foremost I am a woman. After that I am a politician. I will do duty to my country as I would to my children. I will mother it." Below is the male reporter's story about her, beginning, "The Democratic nominee for United States Senate from Minnesota cooks the best ham and cabbage I ever tasted. To make election matters certain all she has to do is invite the voters for dinner." Even the *New York Times* reported on the novelty of her campaign, quoting her as saying, "I do my own housework. I think a woman can attend to her home duties and still participate in club activities or politics . . . " The *Chicago Herald-Examiner* called her "a political Joan of Arc" who was gifted with matchless oratory.

When Anna stated publicly that she was born a Democrat and an admirer of William Jennings Bryan, the *Philadelphia Inquirer* noted, "Whether the unfortunate nominee can overcome these two handicaps is too much for a mere man to say." The *New York Times* wrote that women would eventually be elected to the Senate, but it would not be Anna Dickie Olesen, and that Senator Frank Kellogg's seat was quite safe. They were only half-right.*

On election day the Farmer-Labor candidate, Henrik Shipstead, received 325,372 votes, besting the Republican Kellogg, who won 241,833. While Anna Dickie Olesen received only 123,624 votes, she outpolled the Democratic nominee for governor by almost 44,000 votes. One journal-

---

* Georgia sent the first woman to the United States Senate. Rebecca Latimer Felton was appointed to a vacancy on November 21, 1922, and served until the next day. She was almost eighty-eight years old and the oldest freshman ever to enter the U.S. Senate. The first woman to be elected to the U.S. Senate was Hattie Wyatt Caraway, elected from Arkansas in 1932, losing her seat in 1944 to William Fulbright.

ist wrote of her, "The fact that she was a woman probably lost her at least as many votes as it gained." Years later Anna would note ironically that she was the reason Frank Kellogg became the U.S. Ambassador to the Court of St. James in London, a consolation prize he was given in which he served from 1922–25.*

Her high-profile campaign made Anna a highly sought speaker on the Chautauqua circuit. Her fees increased dramatically, and she began to accumulate the financial resources she had always desired. In 1923 Peter Olesen was named registrar of Carleton College, where he was also to teach German, and the family moved to Northfield, Minnesota. They purchased an English Revival Craftsman-style home in the Highland Park area, and Anna took great delight in filling it with beautiful furnishings. She took no part in college life and did not assume the usual role of a faculty wife, but continued to lecture and to increase her bank balance. She bought and furnished their home while Peter paid for running it. As she said to her daughter, "I can't go mincing around in Northfield as Papa's wife, taking little dabs to the faculty women's clubs." She did accompany him on an extended stay in Germany in 1928 where he studied at the University of Heidelberg.

Anna considered running for Congress in 1932 but decided against it. She was slated to second the nomination of Franklin D. Roosevelt as president at the 1932 national convention, but, when scheduling forced the speeches to be shortened, she instead seconded the nomination of John N. Garner as vice president. For three months, back in her element, she campaigned for the Democratic ticket.

---

* Kellogg served as Calvin Coolidge's Secretary of State and authored the Kellogg-Briand Pact for which he received the Nobel Peace Prize in 1929.

As a reward for her years of political support, she was named postmistress of Northfield, Minnesota. It was not a highly paid job, but it was dependable at a difficult time. In 1934 Roosevelt appointed her head of Minnesota's state office of the National Emergency Council, established to coordinate FDR's social programs. She was the only female state director in the nation. It was the federal administration's top appointment in Minnesota.

In 1936, Anna spoke at the presidential nomination of her good friend, Franklin D. Roosevelt, at the national convention in Philadelphia. The *New York Times* reported of her, "A little woman who could hardly be seen above the speaker's desk, she hailed Mr. Roosevelt as the man who had given courage to the people." In First Lady Eleanor Roosevelt's newspaper column, "My Day," on September 21, 1939, she made note that Anna visited her at her hotel when Mrs. Roosevelt traveled to St. Paul to speak to a women's organization. In her home, Anna always displayed photographs of Eleanor and Franklin Roosevelt warmly inscribed to her. Several state board appointments for Anna followed, and when the agency was abolished in 1942, she was one of only two original state directors in the nation still at her post. Anna Dickie Olesen retired at the age of fifty-seven.

If lives have a second act, then Anna's was to begin far from the icy plains of her native state. In 1949 Peter Olesen left Carleton College to accept a post teaching German at Mercer University in Macon, Georgia. The home in Northfield was too dear to Anna, so they retained it with an intention to return there upon Peter's retirement. It was soon after the move to Macon that the Olesens first met the Burges. By the time in 1951 when Peter Olesen witnessed Chester's contract with the German couple he hired as servants, the Burges and the Olesens were already friends. Anna saw in Chester a "flamboyance," according to her grandson, that was sorely lacking in her own husband. It seems doubly odd that someone who had been so devoted to women's causes would have participated in the ill-advised scheme to marry her granddaughter to John Burge in an arranged wedding. Chester must have had a strong hold on her, but at least she can be credited for having helped her granddaughter escape.

Later in life Anna Dickie Olesen converted to the Roman Catholic faith, and it gave her great solace. The permanent political success she had once sought had eluded her. In fact, she told her daughter, "Every horse has been shot out from under me." She compensated with material success, filling her Northfield home with antiques from the estate of Episcopal Bishop Henry B. Whipple and with items said to be from the castle of the mad King Ludwig of Bavaria. Anna shared with Chester Burge a love of antiques and fine furnishings.* The two understood and shared a need for material affirmation. The Olesens remained in Macon until Peter's retirement from Mercer, when they returned to Northfield. After a long illness, Peter Olesen died on August 5, 1960, while Chester was awaiting his murder trial. Mary Burge had been dead for less than three months.

As soon as Chester was released on bail pending a rehearing for a new sodomy trial, he went right back to Camden, South Carolina, where he had fled the day of his "not guilty" verdict in the murder trial. What was waiting for him there

---

* According to Fritz, at the Burge house on Nottingham, "The large marble urn in the corner Chester always said was a de Medici urn from Italy. It was purported to be worth more than the house. I understood that he swindled it from a Princeton man . . . true? No matter, we are all nearly dead anyway."

that was so important? Anna Dickie Olesen. And, in one of the more bizarre turns in a life that had many, Chester married Anna on April 5, 1961. He was fifty-seven and she was seventy-five. Chester listed the address of his friend Mrs. George R. Cook, Fritz's "Aunt Missy," as his own, and he and Anna were married by the priest of the Roman Catholic Church of Our Lady of Perpetual Help in Camden. They were both widowed, and Chester, no doubt, made no mention of his divorce decades earlier (the same year Anna was Minnesota's Democratic nominee for U.S. Senate) from Laurine Dupriest. She, too, was now dead. Evidently there was no impediment to their being married by a Catholic priest. One has to wonder whether this man of the cloth knew that the groom standing in front of him had recently been convicted of sodomy with his black chauffeur.

Reporters reached the new bride by telephone as soon as the marriage was made public. "I know the whole story about the Macon case," Anna said. "Nothing has been concealed. The other charges are false, and we will fight it to the United States Supreme Court." She also took the opportunity to declare that, "Mr. Burge is one of the finest gentlemen I have ever known." The *Macon News* made note of the fact that, while the new Mrs. Burge "was once prominent in Democratic politics in Minnesota," she "did not take part in politics in Georgia, confining her activities while here to membership in the Mercer Auxiliary and the American Association of University Women." Perhaps as a slight jab at her Northern roots, the paper reported that, "Some acquaintances in Macon felt Mrs. Olesen was not happy here, and one attributed this to the fact that she 'did not have patience with Southern ways.'"

What would lead a woman of Anna Dickie Olesen's accomplishments to marry Chester Burge, eighteen years her junior, tried for his own wife's murder, convicted of sodomy, and awaiting an appeal? According to her grandson, John L. Gerin,* Chester "had what her husband did not. He was a swashbuckling, charming Southern gentleman." Evidently Anna's husband, Dr. Gerin's grandfather, fit Garrison Keillor's stereotype of a Minnesota Lutheran, while Chester "was exciting and flamboyant," according to Gerin. Anna was "a great admirer of his," says Gerin. Asked why she would ignore Chester's glaring faults, he replied that his grandmother, "was a very loyal person to whomever she was committed." John Gerin's sister, Anne, who had been kidnapped and almost married to John against her wishes, agrees that Chester "swept [Anna] off her feet." She says that both Chester and Anna were "the same type that lit up a room when they come in and everybody notices." Of her time as Chester's wife, Anna's granddaughter says, "He spiffed her up. She was a glamour woman there for a while." Together, Anna and Chester would go back to Macon and fight to overturn his sodomy conviction.

On February 5, Judge Long had denied Chester's motion for a new trial. All he could do was wait for the appeals process and keep paying attorneys fees. On May 2, less than a month after Chester's marriage to Anna, the Georgia Court of Appeals heard arguments on both sides of the sodomy conviction. Hank O'Neal and W. O. Cooper represented Chester while Solicitor General Bill West, aided by his assistant, Jack Gautier, argued for the state. The central argument was wheth-

---

* John L. Gerin, PhD, is a highly respected professor of microbiology and immunology at Georgetown University Medical Center. He is a recognized authority in molecular and cellular biology of the hepatitis B and hepatitis Delta viruses.

er Louis Roosevelt Johnson was an "accomplice" as defined by the law. If a witness is not an accomplice, his testimony need not be corroborated. If, however, he is an accomplice, someone or something else must verify the facts to which he is testifying. Although it usually took six to eight weeks for a decision to be announced, the court announced in less than two weeks that Chester's sodomy conviction was reversed. Judge Bill Adams recalled that he recognized Hank O'Neal's handwriting in the court filings, and the defense that was ultimately successful was O'Neal's. The court's decision, written by Justice J. M. C. Townsend with Justices Frankum and Jordan concurring, struck down the state's contention that Louis Roosevelt Johnson participated only because he was on parole and was forced by Chester. The decision found:

> In the present case, if the offense of sodomy was committed as testified by the alleged accomplice, then it was the defendant and no other who participated in it. The difficulty is that the only attempted corroboration of the accomplice that the crime was in fact committed is in the testimony of other persons that the witness, a servant of the defendant, was on certain occasions instructed to go up to the defendant's bedroom after bathing; that he did so; that the door would be closed, and that other servants had been instructed not to enter the bedroom when the door was closed. These facts do not, apart from the testimony of the main witness, raise any inference that a crime was in fact committed. Neither did the occasional presence of used handkerchiefs in the room have this effect, in view of the explanation of the defendant's respiratory trouble.

As to the state's contention that Johnson was forced to commit the acts, the court found that Johnson "testified that . . . he did like it; that it continued for a period of several months, and that he did not object. He said nothing to anybody until over two years later." Finally, the decision asserted that the testimony "tended to show that the defendant was admittedly homosexual, and a part of the testimony . . . tended to show that the defendant considered Johnson . . . to be the same." Perhaps the state could have tried Chester again on the sodomy charge but, without corroboration of Johnson's testimony, it would have been extremely difficult to secure a conviction. Bill West, whom Judge Bill Adams says "was probably thoroughly disgusted with anything to do with Burge," did not seek an indictment to try Chester again. He was a free man.

The house in Macon now belonged to John, and Chester needed a new home. After a honeymoon cruise, John Gerin confirms that his grandmother and her new husband moved to Anna's antiques-filled home in Northfield, where Chester "had about three hundred suits in his closet." He had sheetrock installed over the plaster walls of the Craftsman-style home. It is difficult to imagine Chester in a small community where his wife was the star in the household. Even though the town was only thirty miles from the Minneapolis-St. Paul area, he didn't know anyone there, either, and Anna had earlier made it clear that she had not endeared herself to the faculty wives at Carleton College. If he was going to re-create himself and finally attain the social life he so desperately craved, it would have to be somewhere else. Chester was no longer a wealthy man after his many court battles, and he needed to depend upon Anna to supplement what few financial resources he was able to retain (some of which the IRS was still trying to confiscate). Anna "was not wealthy but certainly had means," according to her grandson, and the two decided to move to the exclusive shores of southeast Florida. It was the perfect place for someone with a bit of money and a lot of ambition.

CHAPTER FOURTEEN

When my wife and I checked into the elegant Breakers Hotel in Palm Beach for her father's seventy-fifth birthday celebration in 2001, the bellman who led us to our room demonstrated how to use the television. He promptly chose only two stations—the Weather Channel and the Financial News Network. What else could there possibly be to worry about while staying at the Breakers? If the sun was shining and the stock market hadn't crashed—both safe bets—it was a good day. In the 1920s and 1930s, the Breakers had a weather guarantee. If the sun wasn't shining for an entire day, your guest room was free. Of course they paid a worker to stand on the roof on murky days and all that was necessary to void the guarantee was his assertion that the sun broke through even for a moment.

The writer Somerset Maugham described Monaco as "a sunny place for shady people," and Palm Beach could, to some extent, be subject to the same characterization. To be sure, there are old Palm Beachers who would never deign to accept the *nouveau riche* who try to claw their way up the social ladder, but that does not prevent many from trying every year.

Anna and Chester were not content to rent a small place to "try out" before committing to one of the most exclusive enclaves in the nation. They first bought a home in Boca Raton but decided to try to climb the social heights of Palm Beach. If they were going to make an entrance, it had to be a splashy one. What better way than to build a new house right on the beach at 206 North Ocean Drive? They knew better than to try to gain membership at such exclusive bastions as the Everglades Club or the Beach Club. It seems the only one Chester joined was the Elks Club.*

Mike Burrows has been an intimate part of Palm Beach for decades. He first began coming down from his family's home in Boston while only a boy and continued his visits throughout his days as a student at Harvard. His father and grandfather donated the land to build a public park in Palm Beach christened "El Boro Park" as a Spanish-influenced version of their family name. Mike Burrows moved permanently to Palm Beach in 1954 and eventually became a successful builder and developer at some of the island's best addresses. In fact, when he was building a new condominium complex, the Duke and Duchess of Windsor made plans to keep a *pied-à-terre* there indefinitely. The Duchess shipped fourteen trunks of clothes to Burrows's address, but she became ill and they were not able to move into the new building.

Although some people recall that Chester pretentiously insisted, once he moved to Palm Beach, that he was a retired French businessman and his last name should be pronounced "Bur-jay," Burrows doesn't remember him that way and actually has pleasant memories of him. "Chester was always *Burge* to me," says Burrows. "He was always very friendly. I had dinner with him on several occasions, or lunches, perhaps both. Even with his wife at least once." I have been the beneficiary of Mike's hospitality, and he is rare in Palm Beach in accepting someone at face value, no matter his background. He is

---

* According to Jack Caldwell, the Macon Elks Club would not let Chester join, so he became a member in a nearby small town, allowing him access to the Elks Club benefits in Macon.

also among the few who have publicly discussed the rampant anti-Semitism he has personally experienced in Palm Beach society. "I have some memory of talking with him about some of the anti-Semitism I was feeling on a constant basis, and his disbelief that such a thing was going on. He seemed the perfect gentleman, and one who was a good listener, as I recall. Not that I recall dwelling on the anti-Semitism subject ever with him; he expressed a Southerner's disdain for such things, and recognized how 'divided' was this community," Burrows continued.

Chester must have asked someone to recommend a good builder, and Burrows was one of the best. "I believe I met him at one of my homes I was building at the time. I think that was the connection. But his friendliness and general pleasant behavior made him a nice friend. He was easy with himself, no airs, no complications I could see. It was a very pleasant relationship, though I cannot say we were that close. We saw one another kind of infrequently during that winter," recalls Burrows. Considering what was to happen, another of Burrows's comments is particularly telling: "Never once did I detect anything sinister about him, or more, about his relationship with his wife. I know she liked to stay at home, and I do recall that he told me she was quite wealthy." That may have been true, but the mortgage on the new house was signed by Chester. The lender? Newbold Hutchinson, Fritz's "Uncle New."

Evidently Anna began to have doubts about Chester once they were living in Palm Beach. According to her granddaughter, Anne, Anna's only child, Mary, began to worry that her mother might be Chester's next victim. It is difficult to know what Anna might have experienced, but in August of 1963

Anna went to Macon to make inquiries about Chester's past. Hal Anderson, who was close to the younger Burges, recalled that Anna "came through Macon and saw John and Jo-Lynn and was just in tears and was frantic. [John and Jo-Lynn] told us she came to see them and was just terrified about Chester." Gus Kaufman also remembered that Anna went to see Dr. Shannon Mays, who had been one of the psychiatrists who examined Chester during the murder trial. He told her, "Go home to Minnesota." The police officers with whom she spoke told her the same thing. Fortunately for her, she went directly to Northfield and did not return to Palm Beach.

At 3:30 a.m. on Sunday, October 7, 1963, Chester Burge was alone in his oceanfront house in Palm Beach when it exploded. "The roof was blown off by the explosion, and glass was scattered in all directions. A neighbor said the blast was heard by residents three blocks away," reported the *Macon News*. Joe Gaffney, who later was Palm Beach's chief of police, was then a police sergeant involved in the investigation. He remembered, "When the house blew up, a patrolman was going by the area. He saw a man running across the front lawn of that house. He thought he had a raincoat on, but it was his skin falling off." Chester was horribly burned and was taken to a hospital where, Gaffney said, "I talked to him right before he died and he didn't want to say anything. He was taking his secrets to the grave."

At the time, Palm Beach police said that Chester had been on the top floor of the "expensive, two-story house" when the explosion occurred, and instead of jumping from a window, he ran downstairs and out the front door. According to the report, "the top part of the man's body was aflame when he was found." In fact, the *Macon News* reported that "the patrolman said he at first thought it was a fireman whose jacket was burning in the stiff breeze, but he discovered that Burge apparently was entirely nude when he ran from the house."

Early reports speculated that the explosion was caused by a gas heater leakage and that is how the event was reported both in Macon and in Palm Beach. I discovered much later, however, that the gas company confirmed that the gas had not even been turned on at the location that was first suspected of being the source of the fire. When Anna was informed of her husband's death, she said the gas heaters had only been installed three weeks earlier. She also made plans to fly to Macon for Chester's funeral service. The only immediate comment from Macon police was that they were waiting for definite identification of the body "so that files concerning Burge might be closed."

The next day's *Macon Telegraph* could not resist leading their front-page story with, "Macon's Chester A. Burge, who made bizarre headlines in life, continued today as an equally sensational newsmaker in death," nor reporting the fact that he had been "turned into a human torch." By that time, Police Sergeant Gaffney reported that before Chester had "lapsed into unconsciousness and died, he was asked questions about the cause of the explosion but . . . he could not help in pinpointing the cause." Those hoping for a deathbed confession were disappointed, also, when Gaffney confirmed that Chester made no comments concerning the murder of his late wife. Palm Beach police asked their peers in Macon to send Chester's fingerprints so they could confirm his identity. Meanwhile the remnants of the house were boarded up against the expected landfall of Hurricane Flora. For more than forty years, no one built on the site. It lay like a gash in the manicured lawns of Palm Beach, a constant reminder of something unpleasant, but not enough to ruin one's day in paradise.

Palm Beach police investigators later publicly confirmed the explosion as accidental, but with details that raise more questions than they answer. The *Atlanta Constitution* wrote within days of Chester's death of "reports circulating widely in and around Palm Beach that there was possibly foul play and that Burge may have been waylaid gangland style." Fire Chief Clarence Teed reportedly "talked to Burge Sunday before his death and was told that something went wrong with the gas heaters in the two-story house and Burge went out beside the garage to turn off the gas at the meter. When he returned, the house exploded." Even absent the question of why the fire chief would have been called to the hospital in the middle of the night to question a horribly burned and dying man, that version of events contradicts the account of the eyewitness patrolman who was driving by at the time of the explosion. There was also a reported deathbed meeting with Chester's attorney, Bruce Jones of West Palm Beach, who supposedly was told by Chester that he "couldn't bring himself to jump out the second-story window and went down through the building to get out." It sounds like a crowded and chatty scene at the bedside of someone who would have been in shock. Macon's current fire chief, Marvin Riggins, is of the opinion that, in the first minutes after the initial shock of the fire, Chester could well have been coherent but his ability to reason and speak would have "deteriorated rapidly." Considering the length of time it would have taken to identify Chester's attorney in the middle of the night and summon him to the hospital, it strains credulity to think that the two had a lucid conversation.

By the next day, Macon's newspapers were openly asking the question WAS BURGE'S DEATH SUICIDE OR MURDER? The third option, an accidental explosion, was not even mentioned until the article's tenth paragraph. Florida police were concentrating on a "business transaction" Chester had entered into about a year earlier with someone in Macon. Sergeant Gaffney would not identify the man but said he was not from Macon and that Chester had "been in touch" with the man "all along." When asked if he knew of anyone who might have wanted Chester dead, Gaffney replied, "A lot of people might have had a reason to." The newspaper story quoted Gaffney in conclusion: "The Palm Beach police, therefore, are probing intensely into the possibility that Burge was either murdered or that he attempted to take his own life, tried to set the house on fire, or, the whole thing was accidental." The police sergeant did add that no one heard Chester make any remark in his final days "in connection with murder or suicide," nor had he done or said anything that would indicate he was considering taking his own life.

Mike Burrows clearly recalls learning of Chester's death. "I remember with great shock when the story came out about the house exploding. In no way did I dream of his involvement. There was *never* a time when he suggested anything that was ugly between him and his wife, or that he was after her money, if in case that was an issue for him. Perhaps we were just never on a page that allowed for that kind of conversation, but it was a total shock to me."

By October 17, there was a new twist to the story. Palm Beach police announced that they were looking for $42,000 worth of jewelry, which was reported to be in the house when it exploded. Detectives were quick to say that "chances are" Chester had put the jewelry "somewhere for safe keeping," possibly in a safe-deposit box, but there was no sign of any jewels in the ruins of the house. As Gaffney confirmed to me years after the fact, "There was a rumor of jewelry in the house, but we never found anything, even a wedding band."

After Chester Burge died at Good Samaritan Hospital, the local obituary noted that he was "from Minnesota. He was a retired realtor, and a member of the Episcopal Church. He was a member of the B. P. O. E. [Benevolent and Protective Order of the Elks]." He had succeeded in re-creating himself in almost every way, but it had been a Pyrrhic victory. Quattlebaum-Holleman-Burse Funeral Home in West Palm Beach prepared his body and the coffin was shipped by railway (at a cost of $47.84) to Hart's Mortuary in Macon. At 5:15 a.m. on Thursday, October 11, Chester Burge arrived in Macon, although certainly not in the style in which he would have thought. The family had first announced there would be a graveside service, but that announcement was rescinded and it was said there would be "no publicity" about a service or his entombment at the Macon Mausoleum in Riverside Cemetery. In typical Burge fashion, the bill for $1,286.34 for Chester's funeral services was not paid to Hart's Mortuary until April 14, 1965, more than a year and a half after his death.

A decade ago, when I first became interested in the Burge case, I visited historic Riverside Cemetery, where I knew Chester was finally "at rest." The very pleasant woman behind the desk asked if she could help me, and I replied that I would like to know exactly where Chester's body was buried (I did not then know that he was in the mausoleum). Her smile quickly vanished, and she said the cemetery did not give any information about that person nor could she even confirm that he was there. More than forty years after his death, Chester Burge was still a toxic subject. There is no marker on Chester's location in the mausoleum, which is barely within sight of the impressive Dunlap memorial in adjoining Rose Hill Cemetery. Even in death, Chester rests only on the periphery of that venerable family he tried so hard to infiltrate.

On October 21, 1963, Anna Dickie Olesen Burge sent a telegram from her home in Northfield, Minnesota, giving her consent to have the Citizens and Southern Bank of Macon act as temporary administrator of Chester's estate. Two days later the Burges' attorneys in Macon filed a petition for Temporary Letters of Administration listing Anna and John Lee as the "heirs at law." But it wasn't going to be that simple. These were the Burges, after all, so litigation and even more lawyers were sure to follow.

John Burge was, by all accounts, handsome and charming. Writer Willie Snow Ethridge met him by chance in the Atlanta airport and described him as "a slim, fairly youngish, extremely handsome, dark-complexioned, black-haired, brown-eyed man" who gave her a ride to Macon in his "shining, low-slung Thunderbird."* By all accounts, John was a lady's man. Even his son smiled when I mentioned that fact.

"Marianne," the woman who was having an affair with medical examiner Leonard Campbell, was very fond of John,

---

* Willie Snow Ethridge, *You Can't Hardly Get There From Here*, Vanguard Press, 1965; p. 62.

whom she liked more than she did his wife, Jo-Lynn. She says, "Not long after his mother's death, he started drinking. Such a deep, stern expression, a haunted look, and very depressed. I never saw him being spontaneous. He never smiled. John was extremely into another world." She was then working on a graduate degree, and John was very helpful to her. "He helped me with hard course work. He never was too tired. In any condition he would help me. I had to have that course to get my master's degree. Without him I couldn't have done it. He could be a very tender person under that façade of depression." Marianne had many opportunities to see Jo-Lynn's interaction with their children, John Lee and Mary-Leita, the latter of whom "was doted on and got all the love and attention her brother didn't." Joe League agrees about John's drinking. John was, he says, "a real nice guy, quiet. He was an alcoholic, of course—drank himself to death. He was a poor old college professor alcoholic. I liked him."

Hal Anderson lived for years with Herbert Herrington, whom he referred to as his "cousin," as if that would negate any talk of their actually being a couple. Herbert had known the Dunlap sisters and was even one of Clara Dunlap Badgley's pallbearers. Hal remembered that Herbert was frequently a guest at Badgley's "Listenin' Hill," which eventually went to John and, thus, to Chester. "Herbert went to some house parties down there and said just about everybody in Macon was invited to houses in the area," said Anderson. "Herbert was around during those years of Chester's life. Clara loved martinis, and Chester always made sure she had one in her hand. She had a huge estate down near Albany named 'Listenin' Hill,' and when she died, Chester got that property. It mysteriously burned down," he continued.

"When John and Jo-Lynn came back to Macon, they began inviting us over and we would go. Usually on Saturday night. Sometimes for dinner, sometimes not. We would spend the evening talking. Jo-Lynn would cook; she was the world's worst cook. Her cakes would stop a battleship. But she was a sweet girl," Anderson recalled. Their evenings had a consistency to them, he remembered. "Every time we were over there they always talked about how they were possibly going to pay the tax bills. There was always something about taxes. And yet they had whatever they wanted. They drove new fine cars. But they were always broke, always broke. I don't know how that happened. There were lots of things we had to guess at." He also clearly recalled the ring that was nearly torn from Mary's finger when she was murdered. "Mary's ring was found under the bed when she was killed. It was about a seven-carat ring, but it was not pretty. Apparently she [Jo-Lynn] got Mary's ring, or John got it. She would wear it occasionally but not often because I think it had bad connotations or whatever. Jo-Lynn got that and, I think, sold it later, because I don't think she still had it. Jo-Lynn had her mother's ring, which was a smaller stone but much more beautiful, so that was the one she kept and sold the other."

During the time that Marianne was seeing Leonard Campbell, they spent an intimate weekend in Atlanta with John and his then-companion. Marianne recalls, "A visiting friend, the wife of a navy pilot, had an affair with him. We all went to Atlanta together to spend the night and had adjoining rooms. She was crazy about him but he cooled. He was put out that she insisted on seeing him." All four of the weekend attendees were married but none to one another.

Although Hal Anderson was fond of John, he found something a bit unsettling about him as well. "John had a cruel streak," he said. "I hated for John to come over here [to the home of Anderson and Herrington] because he had a cruel streak in him, a very cruel streak. He was even cruel to pets."

Once John resettled with his family in what had been his parents' home, he resumed teaching. While he taught at the University of Georgia extension center in Macon, business-man Al Williams was one of his students. Williams liked John but remembers, "He had a drinking problem and, when he would come in [to the classroom], you could tell he had been drinking, but it didn't affect his teaching." Williams also visited him in the Nottingham house where "they had beautiful things."

John had to deal with closing out his father's estate, yet he still was not clear of the debt his mother's estate owed to the IRS. As her executor, in August of 1961 he had signed a promissory note, secured by substantial parcels of property, to the IRS for $200,000 to be paid in sixty monthly installments of $1,750 each.* Now there was his father's estate to contend with, including the unexpected last wife. Chester had never changed his will after marrying Anna, and John had to handle the issue of how the estate was affected by that marriage.

According to her granddaughter, Anne, Anna lent Chester $40,000 to buy the house in Palm Beach. Anna's daughter, Mary, was furious when she learned about the loan, since money was always tight in their family. The $40,000 was all Anna wanted out of the estate. The problem was that, under Georgia law, since Chester's will didn't include his wife, it was void. All his property and assets in the state thus went to his son, John, subject only to a widow's right to take a child's

---

* When the properties were returned in full to him in October of 1965, they had increased in value to $220,000.

share in the Georgia estate or have "dower"* assigned. Again under Georgia law, the widow's dower interest was a one-third estate in all his Georgia property, while a child's share was an undivided one-half interest in all the Georgia property. Either way, Anna was entitled to either one-third or one-half of his Georgia property. Mary had left her estate in halves, so that John and Chester owned equal portions of the property. According to appraisals, Chester's total estate was worth approximately $400,000.

Anna may have married a Burge, but she had not acquired their rapaciousness in the brief marriage. She said to John, in effect, "Give me my $40,000 back and I will walk away." And she did. In exchange, Anna relinquished all her right, title, and interest in either the Georgia or Florida property in exchange for $40,000. Rather than showing relief for her generosity, John and his attorneys then claimed a marital deduction of $82,000 against the estate, claiming that Anna could have demanded that amount as her legal right. In a decision that went all the way to the U.S. Court of Appeals for the Fifth Circuit,† the court denied the claimed deduction, ruling that all that was allowed was the $40,000 she was actually paid. As for the smaller Florida estate, Anna reached a written agreement with John on February 27, 1964, in which she received $10,000 in a year's support, payable in two checks to her attorney.

---

* The right of "dower" was abolished in Georgia in 1969.

† *The Citizens & Southern National Bank and John L. Burge v. U.S., 451 F.2d 221, 1971.* The court found that "the taxpayers herein seek further complication . . . requesting this Court to incorporate into the marital deduction provisions of the law guiding quilled conveyances of medieval times . . . We refuse to harken back to terms and terminologies whose origins are far removed from the modern phenomenon of estate taxation."

Anna told her granddaughter she realized after a few months of marriage that she never could have stayed with Chester. The granddaughter could not understand why Anna did not shed the Burge name after such a harrowing string of experiences, but she never did. Anna Dickie Olesen Burge remained in Northfield, Minnesota, where she died on May 21, 1971, at the age of eighty-six. The lawsuit over the taxation of her marital deduction was not yet concluded. She was buried next to her longtime husband Peter in the Sakatah Cemetery in Waterville where she lived as a child. She is commemorated, without the Burge name, on a monument in the Woman's Suffrage Memorial Garden on the grounds of Minnesota's state capitol.

Back in Macon, John and Jo-Lynn tried to shed the onus of Mary's murder and Chester's unsolved death. Young John Lee had, when a preschooler, been enrolled at Mrs. Duffy's kindergarten, which was considered the best in Macon. Some were surprised when she accepted him as a student, considering his family's reputation. After the murder, things were even worse. Kitty Carmichael Oliver had a children's birthday party for her daughter, Kacy, at Idle Hour Country Club. Several parents were appalled that she invited little John Lee, but, as she says now, "You can't take out on a child what his grandfather did!"

Jo-Lynn became a docent at the historic Sidney Lanier Cottage, and John, in addition to teaching at Mercer and juggling the finances of his many properties, also operated a paint store. Their house was overfilled with antiques, according to several people who visited. Marianne liked John better but remembered of Jo-Lynn, "She could be very warm, though, and was tight with money. At one point their roof was leaking so badly. She had used aluminum foil she had saved and the leaks came directly down onto the foil. This was all over the porch. She never entertained. The house was filled with junk laid out everywhere all over the floor. Stuff I wouldn't have had." Marianne did not like going to the Burges' because, "He had guns in every room in this dark, spooky house."

Filomena Mullis had an unusual vantage point from which to consider the Burges. Her first husband and the father of her children was Leonard Campbell, the medical examiner and friend of John who was having an affair with Marianne. When I first related to her some of my conversations with Marianne without telling her the name of the woman, Filomena immediately named her and said, "Yes, she was very beautiful." I hadn't known she was aware of the affair. After Filomena's divorce, she married attorney Gerald Mullis, who had tried to warn unsuspecting blacks that they were about to lose their houses to Chester. Although they, too, divorced, they remained on good terms.* Filomena did not share her husband's fondness for John. She says of him, "There are some people you just don't like." She also did not enjoy going to the Burge home to visit John and Jo-Lynn, recalling it as "the most eerie house I've ever entered. Everything was covered with dust cloths." She vividly remembers a lobster dinner where every course was served on specialized silver salvers. Marianne agrees about the house. "It was a gloomy, dark house, something off the set of *Psycho* inside. There were huge clocks everywhere."

---

* Filomena Mullis and I served together as elected members of Macon's city council.

Almost everyone, including Marianne, commented on John's increasing alcoholism. She said of him, "He became very sick and alcoholic. Even close to the end I never saw him drunk. He could control himself. His speech was never slurred. His aura was black. His drinking was his suicide." Finally, on August 18, 1972, John Burge died of alcoholism. His son, John Lee, was living on his own and working at the J. M. Huber plant. By the time he was called to the hospital, his father was already in a coma and John Lee was denied the opportunity to say goodbye. John's daughter, Mary-Leita, was profoundly affected by her father's death and the young teenager's speech and reason were adversely affected for quite some time.

CHAPTER FIFTEEN

Jo-Lynn was left with a difficult and rebellious nineteen-year-old son who had already left home, as well as a traumatized fourteen-year-old epileptic daughter. And bills. Lots of bills. Her situation wasn't quite as dire as that of Blanche Dubois in Tennessee Williams' *Cat On a Hot Tin Roof*, but she would have understood Blanche's lament about the box of family papers that was left in her care:

> *All of those deaths. The long parade to the grave-yard . . . Piece by piece, our improvident grandfathers exchanged the land for their epic debauches, to put it mildly, 'til finally all that was left—and Stella can ver-ify that!—was the house itself and about twenty acres of ground, including a graveyard, to which now all but Stella and I have retreated.*

To make matters worse, the house and its contents weren't even Jo-Lynn's. Under the terms of Mary Burge's will, John inherited both his own half and Chester's half of the estate. But at his death the property was to pass to John Lee and Mary-Leita. Her daughter was not yet an adult, so Jo-Lynn could legitimately control her assets, but John Lee was nineteen. In December of 1972 Jo-Lynn filed a petition seeking one year's support for her and Mary-Leita. There was a will John signed in 1962 before his father's death clearly stating that he wanted his wife, Jo-Lynn, to be provided for in every way. But when she filed for the year's support, the form said John died

intestate and, while the will was mentioned, the form specifically said it was not to be probated. The only codicils filed
since that time concerned John's choice of executors.

Jo-Lynn told a friend that neither of her children "could
handle money." By 1976, she had clearly taken control of the
Burge estate. In that year she sold property next to the building site for the Bibb County jail for $24,000, and another prop-
erty to Proctor & Gamble for $38,300. The proceeds were paid
three-fourths to her and one-fourth to Mary-Leita. John Lee
was not mentioned.

Jo-Lynn surprised some of her friends by marrying again.
As Fritz, in an allusion to *Hamlet*, says of that point in her life,
"If it had been in the Middle Ages, I believe that she would
have joined a nunnery. Ah, Ophelia, where is she when you
need her?" Instead, Jo-Lynn married a local architect named
Chester Crowell. And he moved into "the murder house." Evidently, one man named Chester in that house was enough.
As Joe League says of the marriage, "Chester married Jo-Lynn,
and she insisted they live in her house and that didn't suit
him well at all. He was a strong, dominating person, so they
didn't last long, we all knew they wouldn't." Marianne says
of the marriage, "Mary-Leita was in the bathtub—I guess she
was about eighteen—and he [Chester Crowell] walked in on
her. Jo-Lynn got a divorce immediately."

Eventually, Jo-Lynn decided to sell the house and its
contents and move to Atlanta. As Marianne remembers, "Jo-
Lynn cheated her son out of that house. She hated her son."
Hal Anderson agreed. "When Jo-Lynn left Macon and sold
the house . . . all that furniture had been left, all the possessions had been left by Chester to John Lee, not to John and
Jo-Lynn. But she took it with her and the son took out a war-

rant against his mother and they had to get restraining orders against one another. She was then ultimately forced to sell all of the things." I thought Anderson might have been exaggerating, but on a different occasion, Hal insisted he was correct. "Young John took out a warrant of son against mother for taking furnishings from the house that belonged to him." After a great deal of anger and bitterness, according to John Lee he finally was given by his mother one-half the amount Mary and Chester paid for their house when they purchased it in 1948, even though he was legally entitled to one-half of the entire value of the house and furnishings at the time he and his sister inherited it in 1972. He freely admits that he probably would have gone through all the money quickly at that point in his life had he been given the entire amount he was owed.

Lots of curiosity seekers attended the sale conducted by a Savannah antiques dealer. One who became a friend of Mary-Leita recalls a box marked "Christmas ornaments." When the auctioneer started to sell it, an alarmed Jo-Lynn stopped him and took it back into the house. It contained the family jewels, and she had no intention of letting them go. Another attendee, Jack Caldwell, remembers seeing at the sale John Lee, who "had to buy anything at that estate sale. He got nothing [by inheritance]. If he wanted something he had to buy it. His own toys from his childhood he had to buy."

Of all of the figures in the Chester Burge story, in my opinion the one who suffered the most was John Lee. Because of a life-threatening medical problem at birth, as an infant he was taken from his parents to be reared by Mary and Chester. By all accounts, they both loved him. Then, at seven, his beloved grandmother was ripped away from him in a savage murder that happened just down the hall from his own room. It is highly likely that one of the reasons she fought her attacker so strongly was to protect an innocent little boy she loved. It would be no exaggeration to assume her last thoughts were of him. John Lee doesn't remember anything from that night, but he told me he has thought about undergoing hypnosis to see if any suppressed memories might be recalled. I assured him I would be willing to accompany him if he needed support.

Although John Lee might not have understood everything he heard at the time, he must have known that his grandfather had been arrested and tried for the murder. Rumors about the sodomy trial surely must have reached his ears as well. The boy had to withstand the stares of cruel adults and the taunts of children, who were even crueler. He learned about Chester's death well after the fact only from an offhand remark made by his mother.

John Lee longed for his father's attention and his mother's love. By all accounts, the first couldn't show it and the second couldn't find it. He thinks his mother must share much of the blame for his father's alcoholism because "she can just be a bitch." He remembers Louis, the chauffeur, as being "very nice" but admits, "I didn't know then what I know about him now." He admits that his mother cheated him out of his inheritance but says, "That kind of thing seems to be important to her, and I just had to let go of that anger a long time ago." When his parents moved into the same house where Mary was murdered, he had to become accustomed to a family he had known only as visitors until then. He asked me about an older woman named Mrs. Durden he remembers from his childhood who lived with them in the house. He didn't know until our conversation that she was his great-grandmother, Chester's mother.

John Lee has a portrait of old Captain and Mrs. Dunlap and of their son, as well as some family china. He thought about selling them at a time when he really needed the money but then realized that those items were all he has from his family. His second wife died a long, slow death from cancer, and he had to watch it happen. He had tears in his eyes as he related the story.

John Lee now lives only blocks from the house where his grandmother was murdered, and he works as a mechanic at a service station. Although he suffered from addictions and manic depression for years, his life now seems to be on a more even keel. He is a good person, and my single biggest anxiety in writing this book is that the result will cause him pain. Of all the people I've come across in the story, he least deserves it. In a family that would give the House of Atreus a run for their money, he may be the most honest member. As Oscar Wilde said, "What fire does not destroy, it hardens."

Strangely enough, the person least affected seems to have been Fritz Phillips. His candor and affability have been matched only by his graciousness in answering my many questions. He never pretended to return Chester's love and, as he says, "I thought the hotel business needed me and Mr. Burge was the opportunity." He likens his relationship to Chester as "a little like that of the old rich woman who paid the future Mrs. de Winter to be her companion in *Rebecca*. She did it because it was a way of improving her situation, and not because she found her at all charming."

After his marriage and the birth of his children, he "came out with a vengeance," as he says, and moved to Washington, DC. "I dated Audrey Mellon Currier* when her father was ambassador. In Georgetown all these couples went home at 10:00 p.m., then the men went out with one another. They called it 'walking the dogs,' but the poor dogs had to hold their bladders until about 2:00 in the morning." In describing his life in Washington, Fritz said, "All you needed was a tuxedo and a little French and wow!"

In our online conversations Fritz kept returning to a lingering sexual fascination with John Burge. On more than one occasion he told me a story, which I first dismissed as fantasy. With only small embellishments, it rarely varied from the first time he told me:

"I was a first mate on yachts, usually around Palm Beach, Fort Lauderdale, and Miami. I worked with the extremely exclusive families like the Forbeses and the Fords. We moored at the exclusive Bal Harbour Club, where you weren't supposed to live, but we did. Everyone told us all their secrets. My captain was gay and there was this young skinny guy around that my captain obviously wanted so he worked with us for a while. He [the young skinny guy] and I had hot sex in Frances Langford's pool—do you know Frances?—well, anyway, we did and we went back once more but it was too cold to have sex and nothing happened. Anyway, he knew nothing about my knowing Macon or the Burges and he just casually mentioned that he had been John Burge's lover. So you see Chester's son was AC/DC, too."

---

* Her father, David K. E. Bruce, was the only American to serve as ambassador to France, the Republic of Germany, and the United Kingdom. Her maternal grandfather was banker Andrew Mellon. Audrey and her husband, Stephen Currier, were presumed dead in 1967 when all contact was lost with their airplane while flying over a U.S. military installation in the Caribbean.

After all the stories I had heard about John's womanizing, I dismissed any talk of his bisexuality as purely wishful thinking on Fritz's part. Then Hal Anderson told me during another conversation, "John was bisexual. I never had anything to do with him. But every time there was a young pretty man, he would have his hands all over him." Whether it is true is probably irrelevant in the larger scheme of things except as a footnote to Chester's own textured sexual history.

Now seventy-eight, Fritz doesn't venture far from his home. "For an avocation, I raise daffodils. The blooms are sold in season to the New York market, and when I can, I donate them to various garden clubs locally. I enjoy importing new stock although I have most of the same varieties that I had over fifty years ago. I only have less and less land to plant because I am trying to rid myself of encumbrances." When he asked for permission to donate some daffodils to a local church in my honor, Fritz emailed me, "The daffodils are non-denominational. They simply charm everyone." The description could well be applied to Fritz.

After all this time spent with the Burge family and the murder, those who know about my research and writing ask me what I think really happened. Did Chester murder Mary? How? Who blew up Chester in his beachfront home? The universal response to Chester's death is: "He finally got what he deserved." Did he?

My first confession is that I firmly believe Chester had Mary killed. The trickier question is whether he was present. No matter whether the impetus was the cancellation of the trip to Europe with the high school boy, Mary's refusal to give him money to buy the Florida hotel, or a larger wish to spend the rest of his life with Fritz, Mary put a stop to all three. In my estimation, in so doing she sealed her own fate. The fact that she went to Rex Elder's grocery store to pay her bill in full on what was not her regularly scheduled day indicates that she knew something was going to happen. As she said to Elder that day, "I want to get everything in order."

There was a period the night of her murder when Chester might have slipped out unnoticed from his hospital bed and returned, but it would have been very difficult and very painful to achieve. Harry Harris said police timed it and it would have been possible in the length of time allowed. If, in fact, a nurse helped him, it may have been prearranged. In that case, perhaps she was the nurse who worked that night but had already announced her impending resignation. That may have been Shirley, if Lisa Davis's memories are correct. Alternatively, there may have been a nurse who saw Chester out of bed and was concerned about him so soon after surgery, as asserted by Harry Harris. If so, then Rex Elder's conversation with Chief Bargeron about a nurse who was given cash and a new Chevrolet in return for bringing a doctor's statement that she could not testify in the trial would fit that latter scenario.

The most informative conversation I had during all my research about Mary's murder was with longtime deputy sheriff Harry Harris, who joined the investigation at the request of prosecutors who knew the Macon police were not up to the job. Although he was very reluctant to meet with me, he finally did so when Brian Adams, whose grandfather was Chester's defense attorney, asked on my behalf and offered to accompany me. Harris worked closely with Charles Adams and Hank O'Neal when they prosecuted Anjette Lyles. He kept detailed notes from the Burge investigation because he intended to write a book about the case. He passed away with the book unwritten.

First, when asked why Mary put up with Chester's life-style for so long, Harris replied, "She had an easy life except for his abuse. She got used to the money." He was not particularly complimentary about Mary, concluding that she "conjured up enough sympathy from people because he made her look good in comparison." His opinion of Mary was shared by Hal Anderson, who said Mary "was not at all attractive and I heard that she was as bad as Chester was." Joe League offers a kinder view. He says Mary "was such a nice, gentle person. How she could stand to live with him as long as she did, I don't know. She must have just separated herself from him mentally and physically, I guess."

It was Harry Harris who knew about the two men hired at the Jewel Box, a gay bar in Florida, to murder Mary. He even knew at which hotel they stayed while in town. They were the two men who visited Chester in the hospital only hours before Mary was killed. Even though police identified and spoke with them, they were never called to testify. In order to be more definitive about their role, it is necessary to add the most valuable information about Chester's death, which came from two sources.

The first was Joe Gaffney, a Palm Beach police sergeant at the time of Chester's death, who later became chief of police. When I spoke to him in his retirement home in North Carolina, he needed no prodding to remember the house explosion case. It is one that still gave him cause to wonder. Soon after Chester's death, Gaffney went to Macon to expand his investigation and talked with police officers who were intimately familiar with Mary's death and Chester's background. Interestingly, he shares Harry Harris's opinion of both Mary and Chester Burge. He said Chester "was crooked as a snake."

Gaffney "checked into his background and went to Macon to investigate. He prostituted his wife in Macon to sleep with men. Everything he touched was crooked." Gaffney also confirmed that, "The IRS was after him after he died. There was a spin-off IRS investigation."

Gaffney led the investigation into the house explosion in Palm Beach. "You could stand in the middle of where the house was and measure in any direction, and it was a perfect circle. Only dynamite or explosives do that." It obviously was not a gas leak. In fact, he told me that the gas company was furious when police announced a gas leak as the cause early in their investigation. Gaffney "sent fifteen cans of debris to the FBI, but they could never come up with any usable evidence. If we saw a hot spot in the floor, we cut it out and sent it in." He knew this was not an ordinary case of arson—this was a professional hit. "I sent samples to the FBI because the perimeter was such a perfect circle, which would indicate dynamite. The cellar was all that was left of the house. We sifted but never found anything." That included any sign of $42,000 of jewelry that was supposed to be in the house. There was not even a charred wedding band. In the end, said Gaffney, "We looked at the mafia but couldn't prove anything." His conclusion as to who killed Chester? "I thought it was some kind of revenge thing but never found anyone . . . Somebody got him, no two ways about that. That son of a bitch got what he deserved."

It seems obvious that Chester's killer was not an amateur. The most likely people who had the expertise and the proximity to Palm Beach in 1963 to pull off that kind of execution without detection (remember that a police officer was there within seconds and even saw Chester run from the house in flames) would have been a crime outfit such as what Jordan Massee called "Murder, Incorporated"—the branch of the mafia hired for professional hits. That theory may be yet another strange twist in a bizarre tale, but it is certainly possible. If they killed Mary, then is it possible Chester didn't pay them and they were out for revenge? Or did they come back for more money when they realized how much Chester inherited? Or did they just get greedy? The $42,000 worth of jewelry that was supposedly in the house would have been good compensation against any of those possibilities.

Erma Lanneau, whose husband was the first policeman on the scene of Mary's murder, told me, "Chester's money ran out. He had been blackmailed by those men who did the killing and they set him on fire like a torch and threw him out in the yard." The Lanneaus' daughter, Kay Lanneau Putnal, said, "My daddy always thought the chauffeur helped him [Chester] do the murder. Daddy thought he got mixed up with 'the wrong people' in South Florida, maybe money he owed or something, and that along with his lifestyle got him killed." Marianne knew a great deal about Mary's and Chester's deaths because of her relationship with Leonard Campbell, the medical examiner. She concluded, "The men Chester had hired for the killing were blackmailing him. They set him on fire like a human torch."

The other source concerning Chester's death contradicts the first. Hal Anderson remembers that Chester Burge "was despised by everybody. He was a poor relation of a rich family in Macon. That was one thing that was wrong with him. He was involved in every slimy operation in Macon." Asked why Louis, the chauffeur, would have had a two-year physical relationship with Chester, Anderson answered, "I would say he was forced into it. Chester was a repulsive creature. Tiny, mean, ugly little eyes." But Hal thought he knew for sure who killed Chester. He twice told me the following story with no hint of doubt: "One night—John drank heavily—one night he was here. He was often over without Jo-Lynn and the children. Herbert was playing the piano. He [John] sat beside him. He started talking about the murder, and this was right after Chester was killed in Florida. John Burge, sitting right here on that piano bench, said, 'I took care of that God-damned son of a bitch. I did it.' He never said that to anybody else that I know of, but I heard him say that. So he, himself, took care of Chester. He hated him with a purple passion."

While John had every reason to hate his father, this is one story to which I cannot give credence. I am of the opinion that his bravado in making such a claim was a combination of alcohol and hubris. If there is any truth in it at all, then surely John cannot have meant that he personally blew up his father's house. Perhaps it was similar to Chester's role in Mary's death—he didn't perform the killing, but he had it done. Still, I strongly lean toward the explanation of one of any number of professional murder-for-hire organizations. John may well have wished his father dead, but I don't think he had him killed. I think the two men who killed Mary— regardless of whether Chester was there or not—had reason to wish him dead. The reason was probably financial, but who can say for sure?

And what about Louis, the chauffeur? His story on the night of Mary's murder is certainly a strange one. He lived in the basement of the Burge home for more than two years but had recently moved out to live with his new wife. He would have us believe that he left the Burge home between 9:00 and

10:00 p.m. (which would have been within minutes of Mary's return), went home and joined his wife, got up from his wife's bed just minutes before midnight, went to the home of Jessie Mae, the maid, and stayed there until the next morning. What might his new wife have thought of that arrangement, and why wasn't she called to testify or at least verify the first part of his alibi?

I found no trace of Louis Roosevelt Johnson after the sodomy trial. I suspect that he left town rather quickly, and I certainly couldn't blame him. Although I've not come across anyone with knowledge of him after that time, there is a curious footnote about another Burge employee. Dot and Rex Elder knew one of the Burge gardeners, Willie Toomer, who was also African American. According to them, he was very tall, 6'6" or 6'7", and he "was a powerful man. He was 'slow' but not retarded." Years later, they were visiting San Francisco and ran into him there. Says Rex, "I don't know how he had the money or the wherewithal to move out there." He seemed nervous when they spoke with him. It would not have taken much money to relocate someone to another state, and I would presume that's what also happened to Louis Roosevelt Johnson. Someone helped him get out of town.

In the final analysis, I think the Macon police were sloppy, and the prosecutors relied on prejudice and hatred to make their case. They didn't call witnesses they should have and didn't follow leads that might have been productive. They assumed that a jury would convict based on Chester's sexual activities in general and specifically because of his relationship with a black man. It speaks volumes that an all-white jury in Macon in 1960 did not convict someone who admitted that those facets of his life were true. Just as I was surprised to learn that one-third of the jury pool was opposed to capital punishment, I am impressed that a jury at that time and in that social milieu would find Chester not guilty based entirely on facts and not on prejudice. It strengthens my pride at being a ninth-generation Georgian. As juror Willard McEachern said, the state didn't prove what they contended. That certainly didn't mean they approved of Chester. As another juror, William Couch, said years later, "There just wasn't enough evidence to convict him . . . he was burnt up down in Florida. He got his due anyway." That last statement was echoed over and over with many people who were familiar with the case— Chester got what he deserved.

Chester Burge would never have described himself as "gay" even if he played a minor role in Georgia's transformation of the laws concerning homosexuality and sodomy. His conviction was, somewhat surprisingly, overturned based entirely upon the relevant law as it applied to "accomplices" and had nothing to do with any attempt to liberalize Georgia's sodomy statutes. Yet few other states can claim to have played such a pivotal role in that evolution.

Long after Chester's death, sodomy remained a felony in Georgia. In August of 1982, a policeman in Atlanta (named by *Advocate* magazine in 2010 as "America's gayest city") delivered a summons to a young man, Michael Hardwick, for throwing out a beer bottle in a trash can outside the gay bar where he worked. When the officer arrived at Hardwick's house, a guest who was sleeping on the sofa answered the door and allowed the policeman to enter. Looking past a partially opened bedroom door, the officer saw Hardwick and another man engaged in mutual, consensual oral sex. He placed both men under arrest for sodomy, which Georgia defined as including both oral and anal sex between members of the same sex or of the opposite sex. Although the district attorney decided to ignore the arrest and not present the case to a grand jury, Hardwick sued Georgia's attorney general, Michael Bowers, in federal court, seeking to overturn Georgia's sodomy law because he knew he could be charged under it in the future.

The American Civil Liberties Union (ACLU) had been looking for several years for a test case to challenge sodomy laws, and they adopted Hardwick's as the perfect one. The U.S. District Court for the Northern District of Georgia dismissed the case in favor of Attorney General Bowers. But the U.S. Court of Appeals for the Eleventh Circuit reversed the decision, finding that Georgia's sodomy laws infringed upon Hardwick's rights. When Georgia appealed, the U.S. Supreme Court agreed to hear the case with Harvard law professor Laurence Tribe representing Hardwick.

In a sharply divided 5-4 decision,* the U.S. Supreme Court found that the Constitution does not confer "a fundamental right upon homosexuals to engage in sodomy." Justice White wrote the majority opinion (which only applied to homosexual sodomy and not to heterosexuals), finding that any claim that the Constitution guarantees any sort of historical right to sodomy "is, at best, facetious." Chief Justice Burger wrote a separate concurrence that any other decision "would cast aside millennia of moral teaching." The deciding vote was cast by Justice Powell who, it was said, believed he had never known any homosexuals even though one of his own law clerks was gay. Three years after the decision, Justice Powell said that he had been wrong and the Court's decision was incorrect. However, *Hardwick* remained the law of the

---

* *Bowers v. Hardwick*, 478 U.S. 186 (1986)

land. Even though most states did not enforce sodomy laws against consenting adults after the decision, it was still the official law even though some states repealed their sodomy statutes in response to the decision.

Finally, in 1998, the Georgia Supreme Court struck down its own sodomy law that had been upheld by the U.S. Supreme Court in *Hardwick*.* Not until 2003 were the remaining state sodomy laws in the United States invalidated by the U.S. Supreme Court when applied to consensual conduct among adults.† By then Chester Burge had been in his mausoleum for forty years, a wretched soul who was little more than a minor footnote in the jurisprudence of sodomy. By all accounts, it is not a distinction he would have wanted.

After spending almost a decade immersed in Chester's life, I'm still not sure I understand much of him beyond his unquenchable thirst for social acceptance. He wasn't so much immoral as amoral. If he wanted something, nothing and no one could stand in his way—at least not for long. The end always justified the means. Perhaps Hal Anderson, who knew Chester and his family well, had the best analysis of him: "Chester only knew money. He didn't know love. He only knew lust and money, and that was it. An odd little man."

---

* *Powell v. State of Georgia*, 270 Ga. 327 (1998)

† *Lawrence v. Texas*, 539 U.S. 558 (2003)

ACKNOWLEDGMENTS

My first debt of gratitude is to the late Jordan Massee, whom I miss every day. Not only did he first tell me about the saga of Chester Burge, but he entrusted me with the scrapbook he assembled in New York from newspaper clippings sent to him daily by his sister in Macon during the trials.

Secondly, I am deeply appreciative to Fritz Phillips, who was always cheerful, candid, and accommodating in spite of far too many queries from me. Despite his background, or perhaps because of it, he chose decades ago not to hide his emotions and his preferences and in the process became a much more fulfilled adult. I hope his many quotes I have used will not offend him or bring him unhappiness in any way.

Although several sources insisted upon anonymity, I am grateful to the following for their valuable contributions: Brian Adams, the late Hal Anderson, Albert Billingslea, Ed Bond, Mike Burrows, John Lee Burge, Tommy Bush, Jack Caldwell, Dr. Lisa Davis, Dot and Rex Elder, Joe Gaffney, Dr. John Gerin, the late Harry Harris, the late Hattie Tracy King Hartness, the late P. L. Hay III, Jean and the late Dr. Jasper Hogan, the late Marion and the late Gus Kaufman, Leon Kennington, the late Erma Lanneau, Joe League, the late Willard McEachern, Frank McKenney, Buck Melton, the late Filomena Mullis, Gerald Mullis, the late Laura Nelle O'Callaghan, Kitty Carmichael Oliver, Thom Phillips, Carey Pickard III, Kay Lanneau Putnal, Macon-Bibb Fire Chief Marvin Riggins, Ed Sell III, Mary Knight Sheridan, Bibb County District Attorney Howard Simms, Marie Lanneau Stepter, Anne Gerin Warren, Mrs. Ed Wilson, and Ann Dunlap Youmans. I am also indebted to Dr. Ivan Allen, the archives at Wesleyan College, and to the Special Collections Department at the Ilah Dunlap Little Memorial Library at the University of Georgia.

Hugo Vickers has never wavered in his encouragement and support. Jim Barfield offered his valuable historical knowledge as well as his friendship. Phil Comer shared an audiotape of an interview with the late Dr. Herman Westmoreland. Willard Rocker, Muriel Jackson, and the staff of the Washington Memorial Library in Macon were always helpful and accommodating.

My agent, Jason Allen Ashlock, revived my literary concentration as well as my faith in agents, while Keith Wallman was an excellent and enthusiastic editor at Lyons Press.

My wife, Katherine, and our daughter and son, Katy and Martin, have generously given way to deadlines, false starts, and occasional despair. I owe them more than love.

SOURCES

There is no transcript of the murder trial. Had Chester been convicted, the stenographer's notes would have been transcribed for use by the appellate court. Fortunately, there were four newspapers covering the trial—the *Macon Telegraph*, the *Macon News*, the *Atlanta Journal*, and the *Atlanta Constitution*. By relying upon all four, it was possible to re-create almost all of what happened in court. In every case in which I have directly quoted someone, that quote came from at least two of the four newspapers. It was particularly interesting to note the subtle word differences from reporters covering the same testimony.

The sodomy trial was covered in detail only by the two Macon newspapers, with brief summaries in other dailies. In 1960, newspapers did not print graphic sexual details recounted by witnesses other than in general euphemisms. There was an official transcript of the sodomy trial since Chester was convicted and the case went up on appeal. That transcript is missing as are all the evidence records from the murder trial and any written record of what Chester might have said under the effects of the "truth serum." The Georgia Court of Appeals decision overturning the sodomy conviction does include some details from that trial, and those are recounted here.

The official medical examiner's report and the coroner's report, including graphic photographs of the victim and of the murder scene, were taken home by the late Leonard Campbell, the medical examiner, who planned to write a book. In fact, he wrote an extensive outline and several chapters. I have not seen his work, nor would his last wife allow me to see the official reports. At her insistence, I offered her financial compensation, but she deemed it insufficient.

The Bibb County courthouse is full of reams of documents covering everything from Chester's lunacy commitment and first divorce to the Badgley will dispute. Hundreds of pages of wills, real estate transfers, estate inventories, and other legal minutiae are available for perusal, and I am grateful to Dianne Brannen, clerk of court (who was a near neighbor of the Burges), and her staff, as well as the staff of Bill Self, probate judge, for their kind assistance. Judge Bill Adams, whose father successfully defended Chester in the murder trial, was extremely helpful in obtaining pleadings, jury lists, etc., and more particularly in helping me, a recovering attorney, understand their relevance. I do apologize to legal purists for occasionally changing the sequence of oral arguments. For example, normally a summation to a jury is made by one side and then the opposing side makes its summation. It made no sense to follow that structure in a narrative form, so I have taken the liberty of presenting one side's argument and then the opposition's counterargument. In every case in which a secondary source was used, the narrative contains a reference to that source.

INDEX

ABOUT THE AUTHOR

Richard Jay Hutto is a former attorney who served as White House Appointments Secretary to the Carter family and was chairman of the Georgia Council for the Arts. A frequent international lecturer, Hutto travels widely to speak about his areas of expertise. One of the foremost historians of the Gilded Age, Hutto compiled and edited *Accepted Fables*, the autobiography of Jordan Massee, and wrote *Entitled: American Women, Titled Husbands, and the Pursuit of Excess* (with a preface by HI&RH The Grand Duchess of Tuscany), as well as *Crowning Glory: American Wives of Princes and Dukes* (with a preface by HRH Prince Michael of Greece and Denmark), and *Their Gilded Cage: The Jekyll Island Club Members*. He is an elected member of the City Council of Macon, Georgia, as well as a Knight of Malta and a Knight of the Holy Sepulchre.

He lives in Macon, Georgia, with his wife and children.